Student Activity Journal

ACCESS
Building Literacy Through Learning™

English

Great Source Education Group
a division of Houghton Mifflin Company
Wilmington, Massachusetts
www.greatsource.com

AUTHORS

Dr. Elva Duran holds a Ph.D. from the University of Oregon in special education and reading disabilities. Duran has been an elementary reading and middle school teacher in Texas and overseas. Currently, she is a professor in the Department of Special Education, Rehabilitation, and School Psychology at California State University, Sacramento, where she teaches beginning reading and language and literacy courses. Duran is co-author of the Leamos Español reading program and has published two textbooks, *Teaching Students with Moderate/Severe Disabilities* and *Systematic Instruction in Reading for Spanish-Speaking Students*.

Jo Gusman grew up in a family of migrants and knows firsthand the complexities surrounding a second-language learner. Gusman's career in bilingual education began in 1974. In 1981, she joined the staff of the Newcomer School in Sacramento. There she developed her brain-based ESL strategies. Her work has garnered national television appearances and awards, including the Presidential Recognition for Excellence in Teaching. Gusman is the author of *Practical Strategies for Accelerating the Literacy Skills and Content Learning of Your ESL Students*. She is a featured video presenter, including "Multiple Intelligences and the Second Language Learner." Currently, she teaches at California State University, Sacramento, and at the Multiple Intelligences Institute at the University of California, Riverside.

Dr. John Shefelbine is a professor in the Department of Teacher Education, California State University, Sacramento. His degrees include a Master of Arts in Teaching in reading and language arts, K–12, from Harvard University and a Ph.D. in educational psychology from Stanford University. During his 11 years as an elementary and middle school teacher, Shefelbine has worked with students from linguistically and culturally diverse populations in Alaska, Arizona, Idaho, and New Mexico. Shefelbine was a contributor to the California Reading Language Arts Framework, the California Reading Initiative, and the California Reading and Literature Project, and has authored a variety of reading materials and programs for developing fluent, confident readers.

EDITORIAL: Developed by Nieman Inc. with Phil LaLeike
DESIGN: Ronan Design

Trademarks and trade names are shown in this book strictly for illustrative purposes and are the property of their respective owners. The authors' references herein should not be regarded as affecting their validity.

Copyright © 2005 by Great Source Education Group, a division of Houghton Mifflin Company.
All rights reserved.

Great Source® is a registered trademark of Houghton Mifflin Company.

ACCESS: Building Literacy Through Learning™ is a trademark of Houghton Mifflin Company.

Permission is hereby granted to teachers to reprint or photocopy in classroom quantities, for use by one teacher and his or her students only, the pages in this work that carry the appropriate copyright notice, provided each copy made shows the copyright notice. Such copies may not be sold and further distribution is expressly prohibited. Except as authorized above, prior written permission must be obtained from Great Source Education Group, to reproduce or transmit this work or portions thereof in any other form or by any other electronic or mechanical means, including any information storage or retrieval system, unless expressly permitted by federal copyright law. Address inquiries to Great Source Education Group, 181 Ballardvale Street, Wilmington, Massachusetts 01887.

Printed in the United States of America

International Standard Book Number: 0-669-50897-7
(Student Activity Journal)

        1 2 3 4 5 6 7 8 9–P00–10 09 08 07 06 05 04

International Standard Book Number: 0-669-51655-4
(Student Activity Journal, Teacher's Edition)

        1 2 3 4 5 6 7 8 9–P00–10 09 08 07 06 05 04

CONSULTANTS

Shane Bassett
Mill Park Elementary School
David Douglas School District
Portland, OR

Jeanette Gordon
Senior Educational Consultant
Illinois Resource Center
Des Plaines, IL

Dr. Aixa Perez-Prado
College of Education
Florida International University
Miami, FL

Dennis Terdy
Director of Grants
  and Special Programs
Newcomer Center
Township High School
Arlington Heights, IL

TEACHER GROUP REVIEWERS

Harriet Arons
Lincoln Junior High School
Skokie, IL

Andrea Ghetzler
Old Orchard
  Junior High School
Skokie, IL

Lori Miller
Old Orchard
  Junior High School
Skokie, IL

Marsha Santelli
Chicago Public Schools
Chicago, IL

Tia Sons
Old Orchard
  Junior High School
Skokie, IL

Mina Zimmerman
Deerpath Middle School
Lake Forest, IL

RESEARCH SITE LEADERS

Carmen Concepción
Lawton Chiles Middle School
Miami, FL

Andrea Dabbs
Edendale Middle School
San Lorenzo, CA

Daniel Garcia
Public School 130
Bronx, NY

Bobbi Ciriza Houtchens
Arroyo Valley High School
San Bernardino, CA

Portia McFarland
Wendell Phillips High School
Chicago, IL

RESEARCH SITE ENGLISH REVIEWERS

Nicholas Carozza
Bronx, NY

Claudia Estrada
Hialeah Miami Lakes
  Senior High School
Hialeah, FL

Elisabeth Imhof-Ackerman
Edendale Middle School
San Lorenzo, CA

Alice Scruggs
Martin Luther King, Jr.
  Middle School
San Bernardino, CA

ENGLISH TEACHER REVIEWERS

Brenda Custodio
Mifflin Welcome Center
Columbus, OH

Anita Ensmann
J. E. B. Stuart High School
Falls Church, VA

Dianne Grant
Prince George's County
  Public Schools
Capitol Heights, MD

Andy Luu
Sandburg Middle School
Golden Valley, MN

Nancy Maker
Richfield Middle School
Richfield, MN

Jennifer Moore
Chase Elementary School
Chicago, IL

Vicki Olesky
Harvard Kent School
Charlestown, MA

Kristina Robertson
Minneapolis Public
  Schools
English Language Learner
  Department
Minneapolis, MN

Jill Wegenstein
La Entrada School
Menlo Park, CA

Karen Zogg
Lincoln Middle School
Berwyn, IL

Cover Credits: *Foreground:* Backpack, © Photodisc/Getty Images; Library Shelves, © Photodisc/Getty Images *Background:* Photodisc/Getty Images; BrandX/Getty Images; Based on a system of labeling the columns A through J and the rows 1 through 18, the following background images were taken by the following photographers: A3, A5, A7, A9, A10, A13, A18, B1, B2, B4, C4, C5, C10, C11, C13, C17, D1, D3, D6, D7, D9, D14, D16, E4, E5, E7, E10, E12, E13, F4, F6, F9, F10, F17, H5, H17, H18, I1, I3, I4, I6, I12, I17, J4, J5, J7, J8, J9, J10, J12, J13: Philip Coblentz/Getty Images; A16: Sexto Sol/Getty Images; E9: Albert J Copley/Getty Images; F1, J3: Steve Allen/Getty Images; G7: Spike Mafford/Getty Images

Photo Credits: 4 *top* © Eileen Ryan Photography, 2004 *center* © Eileen Ryan Photography, 2004 5 *top right* © Courtesy Library of Congress *bottom left* © Eileen Ryan Photography, 2004 *bottom right* © Eileen Ryan Photography, 2004

TABLE OF

THEME 1: New Beginnings **6**

- **1** The Reading Process 10
- **2** The Writing Process 14
- **3** Active Reading 18
- **4** Understanding Sentences 22

THEME 2: People Like Us **26**

- **5** Reading Paragraphs 30
- **6** Ways of Organizing Paragraphs 34
- **7** Descriptive Paragraphs 38
- **8** Understanding Nouns 42

THEME 3: Becoming Who We Are **46**

- **9** Reading an Autobiography 50
- **10** Reading Graphics and Websites 54
- **11** Writing an Expository Paragraph 58
- **12** Understanding Verbs 62

CONTENTS

THEME 4: Life Journeys 66

13 Reading Textbooks 70

14 Reading Tests 74

15 Writing Reports 78

16 More About Verbs 82

THEME 5: Our Place 86

17 Reading a Story 90

18 Writing a Narrative Paragraph 94

19 Writing a Story 98

20 Understanding Adjectives and Adverbs 102

THEME 6: Making a Difference 106

21 Reading Real-world Writing 110

22 Persuasive Writing 114

23 Writing Letters 118

24 More Parts of Speech 122

Writing Resources 126

Theme 1: New Beginnings

Theme

A. Making a List List 5 words that come to mind when you look at the pictures on page 16. Tell what each of the words means.

1. _____
2. _____
3. _____
4. _____
5. _____

B. Your New Beginning Think about a time when you had a new beginning in your life. In the Web below, write a few sentences about your experience. Try to use some of the words you listed above.

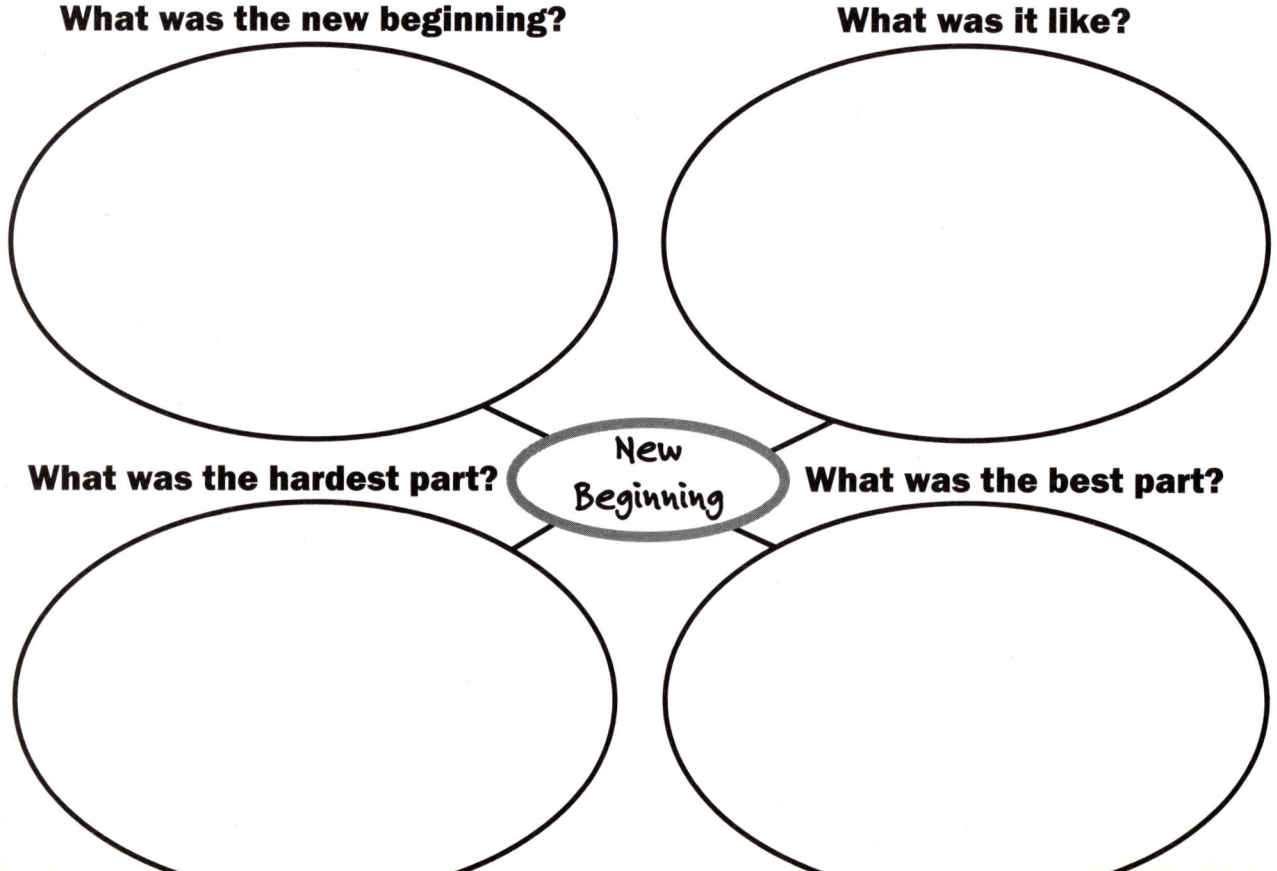

Name _____

FOR USE WITH PAGE 17

Theme 1

Literary Element

A. Definition Chart Complete the Definition Chart below.

Word	Definition	Example Sentence
visualize		
imagery		
image		

B. Using Imagery Try to recall imagery from a new beginning. For example, you might remember the smell of a new city or the sound of a new language. Write a sentence for each of your 5 senses.

1. Taste: _____
_____

2. Smell: _____
_____

3. See: _____
_____

4. Hear: _____
_____

5. Feel: _____
_____

THEME 1 • NEW BEGINNINGS

Name

FOR USE WITH PAGES 18–21

Literature Connection

Making a Web Complete the Web by telling how each poem describes a new beginning.

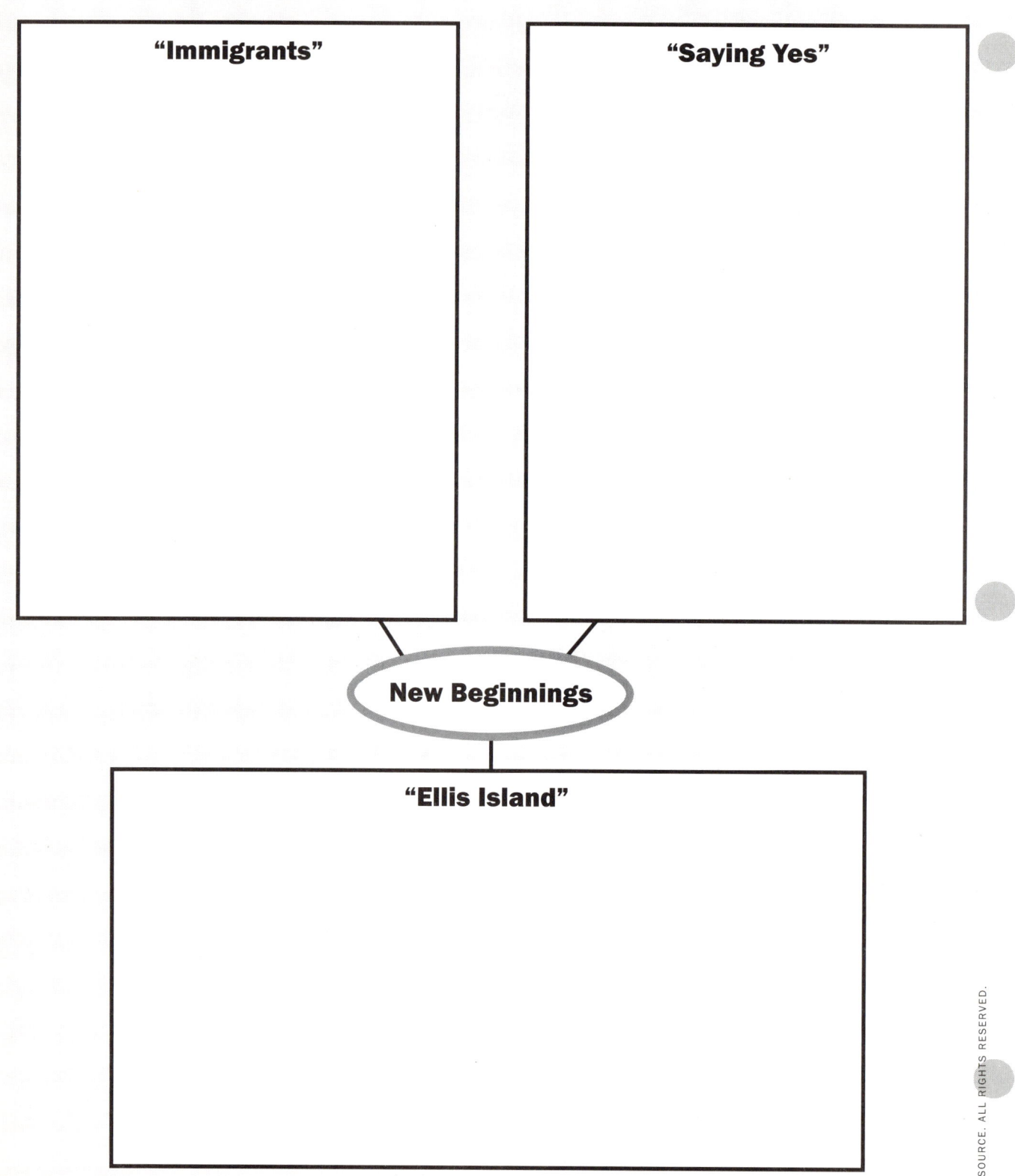

8 ACCESS ENGLISH

Name _____

Theme 1

FOR USE WITH PAGE 22

Learn About Literature

Symbols Think about a common symbol many people would recognize. Draw a picture of this symbol in the box. Then answer the questions below.

What does the symbol represent?

_____

_____

Why do you think we use this symbol?

_____

_____

My Summary of the Lesson

Name _____

FOR USE WITH PAGES 26–33

The Reading Process

My Word List

A. Sequence Chart Fill in the Sequence Chart with the words *purpose, preview,* and *plan*. Put the steps in the right order.

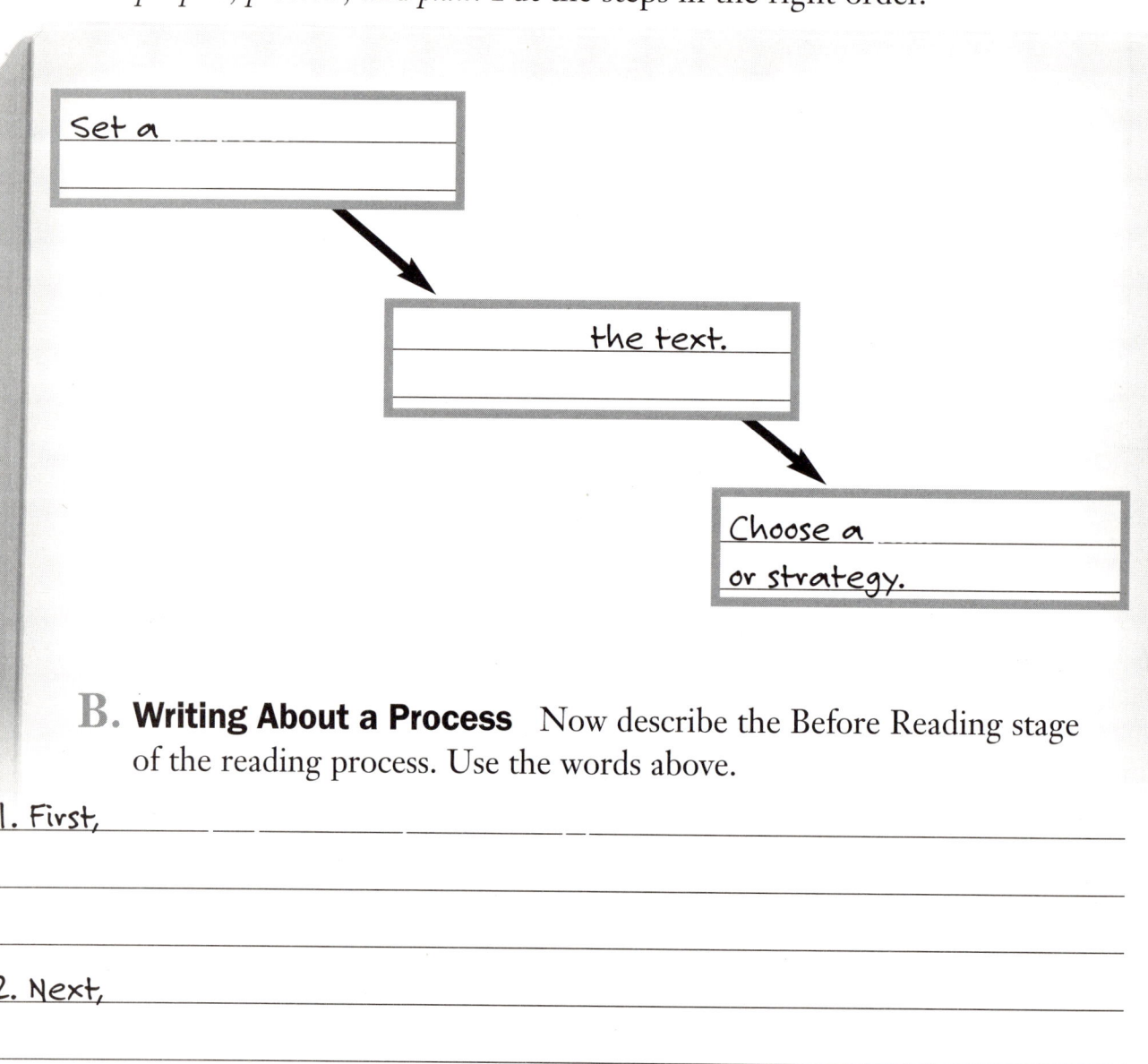

[Set a _____]

[_____ the text.]

[Choose a _____ or strategy.]

B. Writing About a Process Now describe the Before Reading stage of the reading process. Use the words above.

1. First, _____

_____

_____

2. Next, _____

_____

_____

3. Then, _____

_____

_____

Name _____

FOR USE WITH PAGE 27

Lesson 1

Skill Building

A. Taking Notes Reread "Immigrants" on page 18 of *ACCESS English*. Write down your favorite quote from the poem. Tell what you like about it in the Double-entry Journal below.

Favorite Quote	What I Like About It

B. Writing Sentences Write at least two sentences about what you think the quote means.

_____
_____
_____
_____
_____
_____
_____

Name _____

FOR USE WITH PAGES 28–33

My Study Notes

A. Study Skill: Outlining the Lesson Complete this outline for the steps in the reading process. Use the headings in Lesson 1 of *ACCESS English*.

1. Before Reading
   a. Set a Purpose
   b. _____
   c. _____
2. During Reading
   a. Read with a Purpose
   b. _____
3. After Reading
   a. Pause and Reflect
   b. _____
   c. _____

B. Key Details Use the Word Bank to complete these sentences. Reread pages 28–33 in *ACCESS English* if you need help.

Word Bank
text
details
figure out
organize
reread

1. Careful reading means paying attention to _____.
2. A preview can help you _____ what the book will be about.
3. As you read, go back and _____ any difficult parts.
4. Taking notes will help you _____ your ideas.
5. Use the reading process to make reading any _____ easier.

Lesson 1

Name

FOR USE WITH PAGE 34

Showing What I Know

Explaining Draw a line from each step of the reading process to its explanation.

Set a purpose •	• Figure out a strategy for reading the text.
Preview •	• Look for information and take notes.
Plan •	• Ask yourself, "Why am I reading this?"
Read with a purpose •	• Look at the book cover, table of contents, headings, and photos.
Connect •	• Read the text again to answer questions you have.
Reflect •	• Write about what you read to keep track of ideas.
Reread •	• Think about how the reading is like part of your life.
Remember •	• Think about what you learned.

My Summary of the Lesson

LESSON 1 • THE READING PROCESS   13

The Writing Process

My Word List

A. Definition Chart Complete the Definition Chart below. Use the word to write a sentence about the writing process in the last column.

Word	Definition	Example Sentence
organize		
audience		
revise		
draft		
brainstorm		

B. Sentence Frame Use the words in your Definition Chart to complete the paragraph below.

Writing a paper is not hard if you know how to start. Before you write your paper, _____ some ideas on your topic. A good way to _____ your thoughts is to write them down. Writing a _____ means putting your ideas on paper without worrying about how it looks. You can always _____ it later. You should also think about who will read your paper or hear you read it. Your _____ may include your teacher and your class.

Name _____

FOR USE WITH PAGE 39

Lesson 2

Skill Building

A. Writing for an Audience Tell about a kind of writing you could write for each audience. In the last column, write one reason for that kind of writing.

Audience	Kind of Writing	Purpose
My English class		
My graduating class		
A friend who lives far away		

B. Writing Sentences Imagine you were asked to write for the school newspaper. Write a few sentences about a topic that interests you. Then tell who the audience for your writing would be.

_____
_____
_____
_____
_____

Audience: _____

LESSON 2 • THE WRITING PROCESS   **15**

Name _____

FOR USE WITH PAGES 40–45

My Study Notes

A. Study Skill: Outlining the Lesson Use the headings in Lesson 2 of *ACCESS English* to complete this outline for the steps in the writing process.

1. Prewrite _____
    a. _____
    b. _____
    c. _____
2. Write a Draft _____
    a. _____
    b. _____
3. Revise the Draft _____
4. _____
5. _____

B. Key Details Use the Word Bank to complete these sentences.

1. Every sentence you write should begin with a _____.

2. Every sentence ends with some kind of end _____.

3. Some words have the same sound, but different _____.

4. _____ your paper will help you find mistakes.

5. Part of using correct _____ is making sure you use the right word.

Word Bank
editing
grammar
punctuation
spellings
capital letter

16 ACCESS ENGLISH

Name _____

Lesson 2

FOR USE WITH PAGE 46

Showing What I Know

A. **Summarizing** Use the Summary Organizer below to help you summarize the steps in the writing process.

> **Subject:** What are the steps in the writing process?
> **Important Information:**
> _____
> _____
> _____
> _____
> _____
> _____

B. **Writing a Summary** In your own words, summarize the writing process. Use the words *first*, *then*, *next*, *after that*, and *finally* to help you explain.

First, _____

Then, _____

Next, _____

After that, _____

Finally, _____

My Summary of the Lesson

LESSON 2 • THE WRITING PROCESS 17

Active Reading

My Word List

A. Definition Chart Complete the Definition Chart below.

Word	Definition
mark	
question	
react	
predict	
visualize	
clarify	

B. Sentence Frame Use the words in your Definition Chart to complete these sentences.

1. Active readers _____ and connect to what they are reading.
2. Don't be afraid to _____ something you do not understand.
3. If you _____ what you are reading, it seems more real to you.
4. As you read, _____ what will happen next.
5. Even if you think you understand what something means, asking questions will help you _____ the text.
6. _____ the important parts of the text to help you remember them.

Name _____

FOR USE WITH PAGE 51

Skill Building

A. Close Reading Carefully read the lines from "Ellis Island" on page 54 of *ACCESS English*. In the space below, copy the lines from the poem. Then tell what you think they mean.

from "Ellis Island"	What I Think It Means

B. Drawing a Picture Draw a picture that shows what you visualize when reading "Ellis Island."

Name _____

FOR USE WITH PAGES 52–57

My Study Notes

A. Study Skill: Using Key Word or Topic Notes Explain what each of the steps for active reading means.

Key Words or Topics	Notes
take notes	
react and connect	
make judgments	
draw conclusions	
compare and contrast	

B. Key Details Use the Word Bank to complete this paragraph about active reading.

Active reading is more than just looking at the words on a page. Active readers _____ carefully about what they are reading. Active reading means forming _____ about what the writer is saying or what is happening in the text. These ideas come from the way the text makes the reader _____. Active readers also give _____ why they feel that way. They _____ their ideas by explaining why or how they came to those conclusions.

Word Bank
reasons
feel
opinions
think
support

20 ACCESS ENGLISH

Name _____

Lesson 3

FOR USE WITH PAGE 58

Showing What I Know

A. Responding Reread "Immigrants" on page 49 of *ACCESS English*. Choose a part of the poem that interests you. Write it on the left side of the Double-entry Journal below. Then complete the right side.

Quote from Poem	Two Things I'd Like To Say About the Quote

B. Writing a Paragraph Write a short paragraph explaining ways that "Immigrants" connects to your life.

_____
_____
_____
_____
_____

My Summary of the Lesson

LESSON 3 • ACTIVE READING **21**

Understanding Sentences

My Word List

Working with Words Use pages 62–63 to label the underlined sentence parts. Use *subject*, *predicate*, *phrase*, or *clause*. Then explain your choice.

1. _____ Joseph Bruchac writes about his Native-American culture.

   Reason: _____
   _____
   _____

2. _____ When he was growing up, Bruchac wanted to learn more about his ancestors.

   Reason: _____
   _____
   _____

3. _____ Native Americans hunted buffalo.

   Reason: _____
   _____
   _____

4. _____ Bruchac's stories teach everyone about his ancestors' history.

   Reason: _____
   _____
   _____

Name _____

FOR USE WITH PAGE 63

Lesson 4

Skill Building

A. Combining Sentences Combine each pair of sentences into one sentence.

1. The National Museum of the American Indian opened. It opened in 2004.

   _____

   _____

2. The museum is near the U.S. Capitol building. It is in Washington, D.C.

   _____

   _____

3. When the museum opened, 20,000 Native Americans marched to the building to celebrate. They came from all over the world.

   _____

   _____

4. At the museum, you can learn about Native Americans from North America. You also can learn about Native Americans from Central and South America.

   _____

   _____

B. Writing Compound Sentences Now write a compound sentence about something you have always wanted to learn about. Use a connecting word, such as *but, or, and,* or *yet*.

_____

_____

_____

_____

LESSON 4 • UNDERSTANDING SENTENCES   23

Name

FOR USE WITH PAGES 64–69

My Study Notes

A. Study Skill: Using Key Word or Topic Notes Use what you learned from pages 64–69 in *ACCESS English* to write notes about each kind of sentence below.

Key Words or Topics	Notes
statement	
command	
exclamation	
question	

B. Key Details Use the Word Bank to complete these paragraphs.

A subject, an action, and all the words used to _____ them form one complete idea. A _____ clause adds information to your sentence but doesn't express a complete thought. A complete thought within a sentence is an _____ clause.

Writing a good sentence is also about avoiding mistakes. A sentence _____ is missing either a subject or a predicate. More than one sentence put together without any punctuation is called a _____ sentence.

Word Bank
independent
run-on
modify
fragment
dependent

Name _____

Lesson 4

FOR USE WITH PAGE 70

Showing What I Know

A. Synthesizing Use *Lasting Echoes* on page 61 of *ACCESS English* to complete this Details and Statement Organizer.

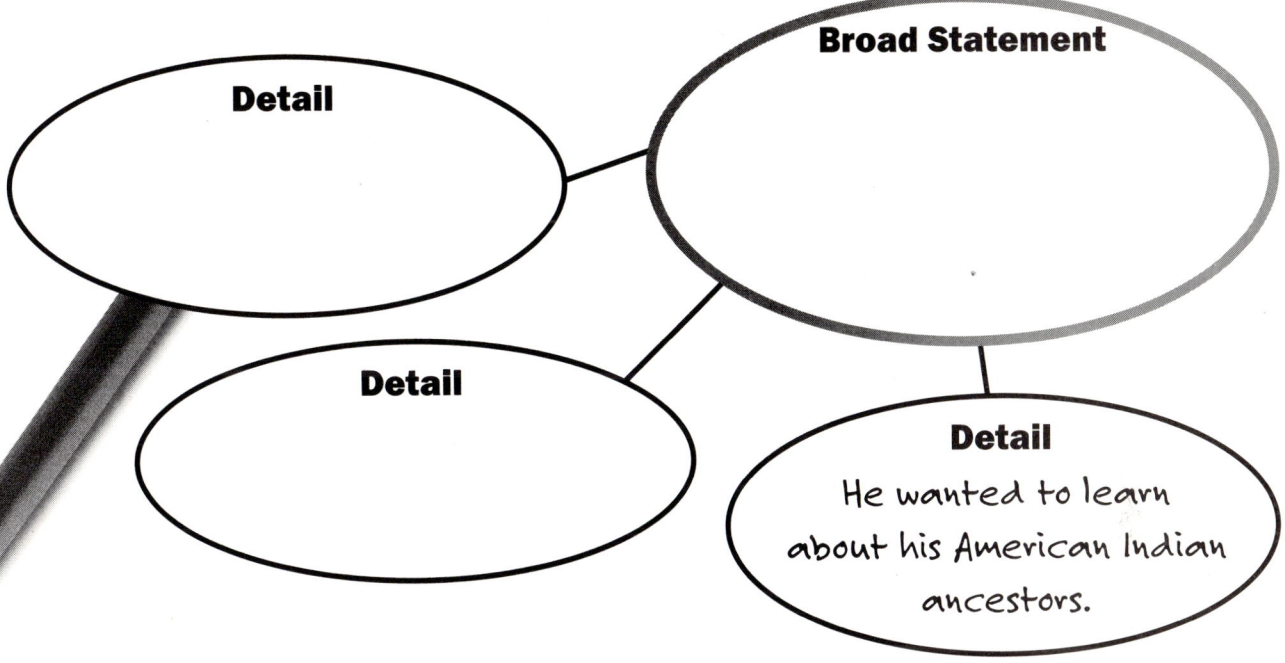

Detail: He wanted to learn about his American Indian ancestors.

B. Writing Sentences Synthesize your ideas from the Details and Statement Organizer into 2–3 sentences about *Lasting Echoes*.

_____
_____
_____
_____
_____

My Summary of the Lesson

LESSON 4 • UNDERSTANDING SENTENCES

Name

FOR USE WITH PAGE 72

Theme 2: People Like Us

Theme

A. Listing Reasons Look at the photos on page 72 of *ACCESS English*. Pick the photo that reminds you most of you or your family. Why did you pick that photo? List reasons why it reminds you of you or your family.

_____
_____
_____
_____
_____
_____
_____
_____

B. Making a Web Think about a time you tried to make friends with a group. Who were the people? What were 3 things you did to get to know them? Answer these questions by completing the Web.

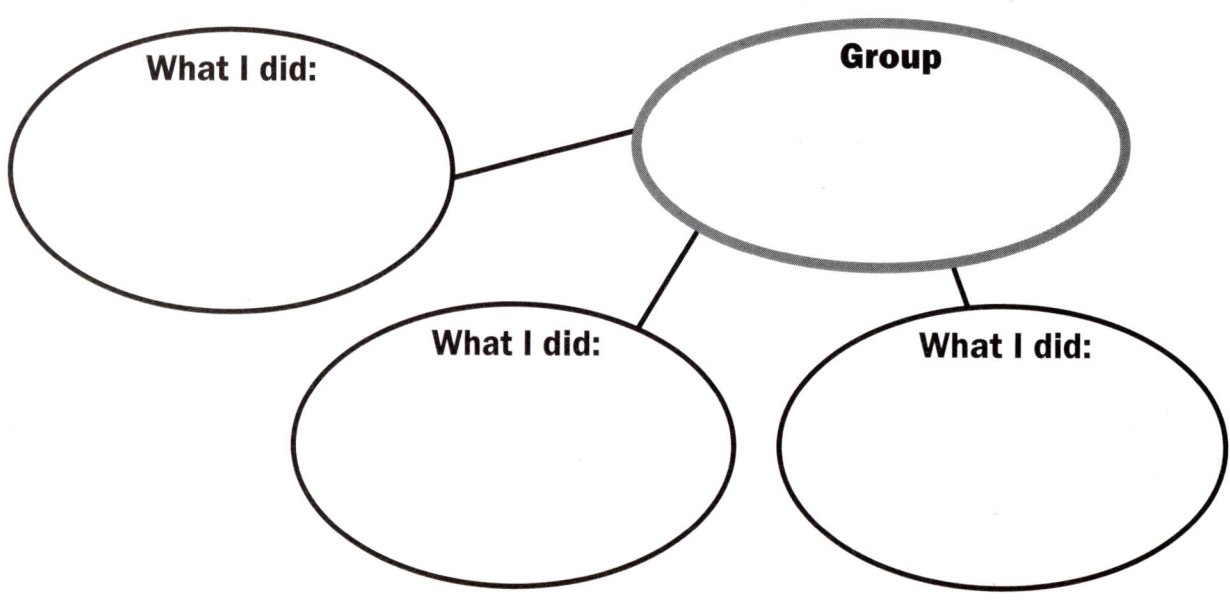

26 ACCESS ENGLISH

Name

FOR USE WITH PAGE 73

Literary Element

A. Definition Chart

Complete the Definition Chart below.

Word	Definition	Example Sentence
tone		
mood		

B. Writing a Description

Think about a friend or family member who means a lot to you. Write a description of how this person makes you feel. Make sure your tone shows the reader how you feel about the person. Think about the mood you are trying to create.

Literature Connection

Making a Web In *The House on Mango Street*, Cathy describes different people she knows. Complete the Web by listing 4 of these people and her opinion of them.

1. Name:
Cathy's Opinion:

2. Name:
Cathy's Opinion:

People Cathy Knows

3. Name:
Cathy's Opinion:

4. Name:
Cathy's Opinion:

Name _____

Theme 2

FOR USE WITH PAGE 78

Learn About Literature

Style Read Cisneros's paragraph below about Cathy. Then rewrite the paragraph in *your* style. What would you say about having Cathy for a friend?

> "You want a friend, she says. Okay, I'll be your friend. But only till next Tuesday. That's when we move away. Got to. Then as if she forgot I just moved in, she says the neighborhood is getting bad."

My Summary of the Lesson

THEME 2 • PEOPLE LIKE US 29

Reading Paragraphs

My Word List

A. **Word Web** Complete the Word Web about paragraphs. Fill in the meaning or definition of each term.

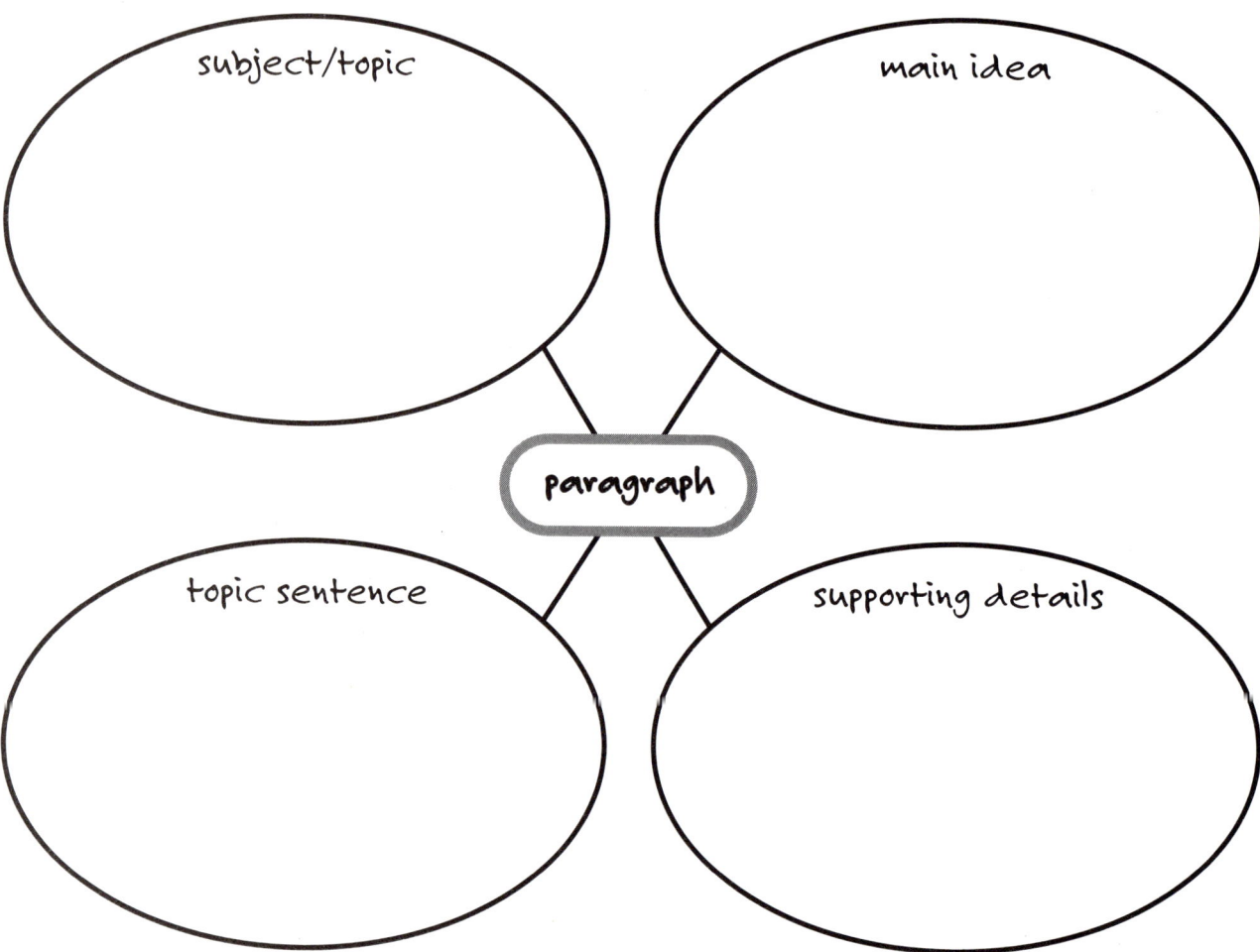

B. **Parts of a Paragraph** Read the paragraph below. Draw a box around the topic. Circle the topic sentence. Underline a supporting detail.

Moving to a new place is never easy. Esperanza knows all about moving and why it's difficult. She's moved to so many different places that she can't even remember the names of all the streets she has lived on. Every time she moves somewhere new, she has to start all over again and make new friends.

Skill Building

A. **Drawing Conclusions** Use the facts below to draw conclusions.

1. **Fact:** It is the first day of school.

   Fact: A girl asks you where the main office is.

   Fact: You have never seen her before.

   Conclusion: _____

2. **Fact:** Your father has an interview for a new job.

   Fact: He comes home smiling.

   Fact: He says he is taking the family out to celebrate.

   Conclusion: _____

3. **Fact:** Your mother is making your grandmother's favorite food.

   Fact: Your little brother is wearing a tie.

   Fact: An extra place is set at the dinner table.

   Conclusion: _____

B. **Writing Sentences** Now write about a time when you came to a conclusion. Include at least two details.

_____
_____
_____
_____
_____
_____
_____
_____

Name _____

FOR USE WITH PAGES 84–89

My Study Notes

A. Study Skill: Reading Paragraphs Answer these questions about how to read a paragraph. Read pages 84–89 in *ACCESS English* if you need help.

1. What are the two main things you need to find out about a paragraph?
   _____ and _____

2. What are 3 ways to find the subject of a paragraph?
   _____
   _____

3. What are the two kinds of main ideas?
   _____ and _____

4. What are the 3 steps for finding an implied main idea?
   _____
   _____

5. What is an inference? _____
   _____

B. Key Details Use the Word Bank to complete these sentences.

1. Keeler, Paulina, Loomis, and Mango Street are _____ of the many places Esperanza has lived.

2. It is a _____ that Cathy lives in a house with many cats.

3. Esperanza gives _____ about the cats to help you picture what it's like at Cathy's house.

4. Esperanza is able to _____ from the way Cathy talks about her family that Cathy thinks she is better than Esperanza.

5. When she spoke about her name, Esperanza _____ that she and her grandmother are strong women.

Word Bank
implied
infer
fact
examples
details

32 ACCESS ENGLISH

Name

Lesson 5

FOR USE WITH PAGE 90

Showing What I Know

Evaluating Read the paragraph below. Then complete the Main Idea Organizer.

I was really nervous on my first day of school. My first class was math. I worried that I would not understand everything my teacher said. My teacher's name was Mr. Espada. I told him I was nervous. He was very nice. He told me he would explain anything that was confusing. I got an A in his class.

Main Idea

Important Ideas	Unimportant Ideas

My Summary of the Lesson

LESSON 5 • READING PARAGRAPHS 33

Ways of Organizing Paragraphs

My Word List

A. Definition Chart Complete the Definition Chart below.

Word	Definition	Example Sentence
organize		
order		
visualize		
support		
contrasts		

B. Sentence Frame Use the words in the Definition Chart to complete these sentences.

1. Time _____ tells when something happens.
2. Details _____ a main idea.
3. There are 5 ways to _____ paragraphs.
4. _____ what you read to help you understand it better.
5. My report _____ the two poems we read in class.

Name _____

Lesson 6

FOR USE WITH PAGE 95

Skill Building

A. Visualizing Read the selections from "Amigo Brothers" on pages 96–99 of *ACCESS English*. Then fill in the Character Map with details about Felix or Antonio.

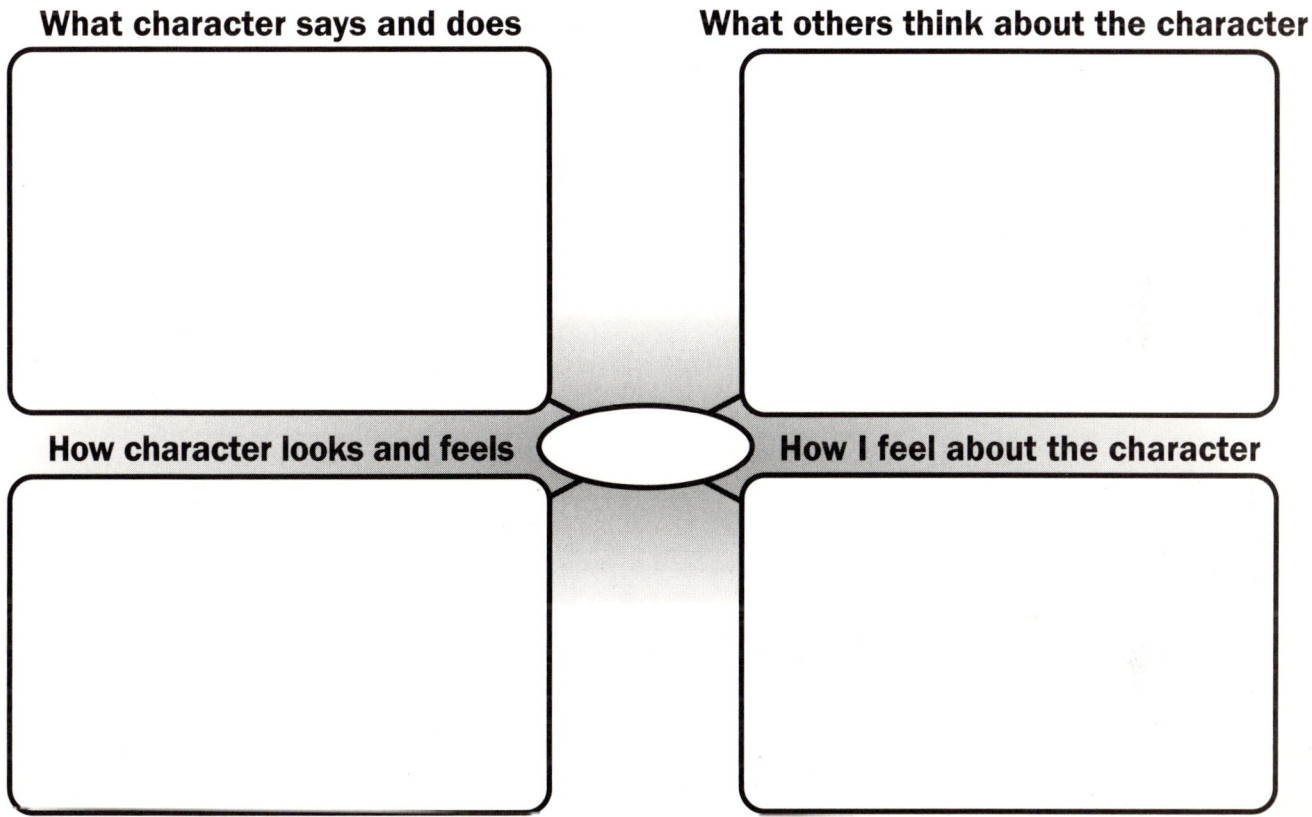

What character says and does

What others think about the character

How character looks and feels

How I feel about the character

B. Drawing a Picture Use your Character Map to help you visualize the character. Use the details from your Character Map to help you draw a picture of what you think he looks like.

LESSON 6 • WAYS OF ORGANIZING PARAGRAPHS 35

Name _____

FOR USE WITH PAGES 96–101

My Study Notes

A. **Study Skill: Using Key Word or Topic Notes** Explain the 5 ways a paragraph can be organized. Use pages 96–101 of *ACCESS English* if you need help.

Key Words or Topics	Notes
compare and contrast order	
order of importance	
time order	
location order	
cause and effect order	

B. **Key Details** Fill in the blanks with the type of organization used in these sentences.

1. _____ To make a cake, first mix the ingredients. Then, bake the cake in the oven.

2. _____ Cats and dogs make good pets, but they are very different. Most dogs do what you say. Cats do what they want.

3. _____ My grandmother was born in Cambodia. Most of her family immigrated to Chicago. Chicago is where she met my grandfather.

4. _____ I was driving my car too fast while it was raining. The car in front of me stopped suddenly. I tried to stop, but I hit the car.

5. _____ I won a talent contest at school! All my friends were in it. Juan did a dance. The dance made me laugh.

Name _____

Lesson 6

FOR USE WITH PAGE 102

Showing What I Know

A. Identifying Use the Venn Diagram to identify the things that are alike and the things that are different between you and a friend.

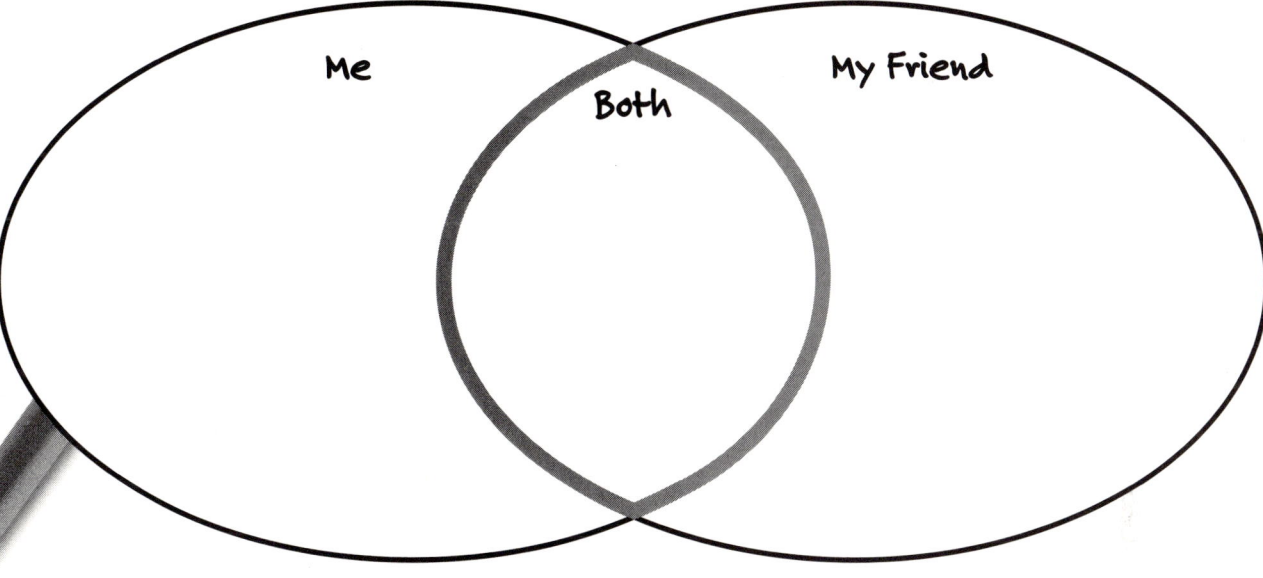

B. Writing Sentences Now use the details from the Venn Diagram to write a few sentences. Use compare and contrast order to identify the things that are alike and different between you and your friend.

_____
_____
_____
_____
_____

My Summary of the Lesson

LESSON 6 • WAYS OF ORGANIZING PARAGRAPHS

Descriptive Paragraphs

My Word List

A. **Making a Web** Define these terms about descriptive paragraphs.

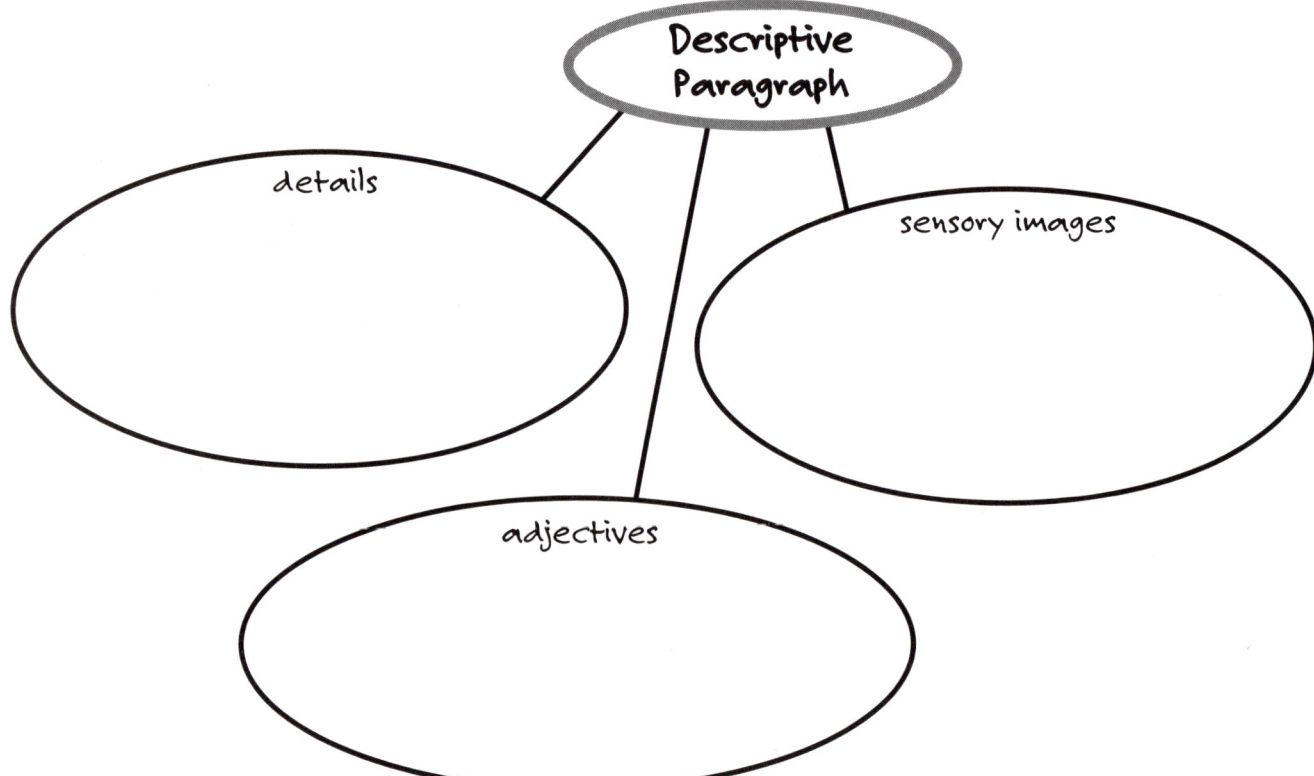

B. **Identifying Terms** Read the descriptive paragraph below about Cobble's Knot from *Maniac Magee*. Use the terms from the Web to identify the underlined parts.

"To the ordinary person, Cobble's Knot was about as friendly as a nest of yellowjackets. Besides the tangle itself, there was the weathering of that first year, when the Knot hung outside and became (1) <u>hard as a rock</u>. (2) <u>You could barely make out the individual strands.</u> It was (3) <u>grimy, moldy, crusted</u> over."

1. _____
2. _____
3. _____

Name _____

FOR USE WITH PAGE 107

Lesson 7

Skill Building

A. Choosing Words Carefully Rewrite these sentences to replace the overused adjective that is underlined with a more descriptive one.

1. That movie was <u>funny</u>. _____

2. This pizza is <u>good</u>. _____

3. My new teacher is <u>nice</u>. _____

4. It is <u>cold</u> outside. _____

B. Writing Descriptive Sentences For each adjective, find a more descriptive one. Then use it in a sentence.

1. sad _____

2. boring _____

3. fun _____

4. fast _____

5. smart _____

6. big _____

LESSON 7 • DESCRIPTIVE PARAGRAPHS 39

Name

FOR USE WITH PAGES 108–113

My Study Notes

A. Study Skill: Outlining the Lesson Use the headings from pages 108–113 in *ACCESS English* to complete the outline about writing descriptive paragraphs.

1. Choose a _____
2. Decide on the _____
3. Add _____
4. Use clear _____
5. Create _____

B. Key Details Choose the descriptive word from the Word Bank that best fits the sentence.

1. The _____ giant tried to catch Jorge but couldn't.
2. I tried to peek inside the old shed, but the _____ windows made it impossible to see anything.
3. My little brother loves to jump on his new bed because it is so _____.
4. The _____ stray dog knocked over the garbage can while looking for his dinner.
5. As people heard news of the president's death, the room was filled with a _____ silence.

Word Bank
springy
grimy
stunned
scraggly
lunging

Name _____

FOR USE WITH PAGE 114

Showing What I Know

A. Describing Choose a subject to write about and describe. Use the Paragraph Organizer to help you brainstorm the main idea, details, adjectives, and images you will use in your descriptive paragraph.

Main Idea:

Details	Adjectives	Sensory Images

B. Writing a Paragraph Now use the Paragraph Organizer to write a descriptive paragraph about the subject you chose.

_____
_____
_____
_____
_____

My Summary of the Lesson

Understanding Nouns

My Word List

A. Definition Chart Complete the Definition Chart below.

Word	Definition	Examples
noun		
proper noun		
common noun		
singular noun		
plural noun		

B. Identifying Nouns Tell whether the underlined word is a proper noun or a common noun. If it is a common noun, tell whether it is plural or singular.

1. _____ The Civil Rights movement of the 1960s produced many strong <u>leaders.</u>

2. _____ <u>Martin Luther King, Jr.,</u> gave a famous speech about segregation called "I have a dream."

3. _____ The speech helped many <u>people</u> see that segregation was wrong.

4. _____ Dr. King gave the speech on the steps of the <u>Lincoln Memorial.</u>

5. _____ Many people think of Martin Luther King, Jr., as a <u>hero.</u>

Skill Building

A. Using Proofreader's Marks   Use proofreader's marks to correct these sentences.

1. In 1955 rosa parks refused to to give up her bus Seat to a white Passenger

2. parks was arrested because She disobeyed the law law

3. the law ordered African americans to sit at the back of the Bus.

4. parks' arrest prompted the 1955 montgomery buss boycott in alabama

5. The boycott was the the Start of the civil rights movement.

B. Writing Sentences   Now rewrite the sentences to include the changes made by the proofreader's marks.

1. _____

2. _____

3. _____

4. _____

5. _____

Name _____

FOR USE WITH PAGES 120–125

My Study Notes

A. Study Skill: Outlining the Lesson Complete the outline of Lesson 8 below. Refer to pages 120–125 in *ACCESS English* if you need help.

1. Common and Proper Nouns
2. Count Nouns
   a. _____
   b. Plural Nouns
   c. _____
3. _____
4. Words That Show Ownership
   a. _____
   b. Plural Possessive Nouns
   c. Other Plural Possessive Nouns

B. Key Details Use the words in the Word Bank to complete these sentences.

Word Bank
ownership
specific
irregular
memorize
apostrophes

1. The words *mice* and *feet* are the _____ plural forms of *mouse* and *foot*.
2. _____ examples of noncount nouns are *ice* and *oil*.
3. _____ are often used with plural possessive words.
4. Possessive nouns are words that show _____.
5. My English teacher asked us to _____ our favorite poem and recite it to the class.

Name _____

Showing What I Know

A. Analyzing Use the Web to organize facts you know about Rosa Parks, Martin Luther King, Jr., or another civil rights leader.

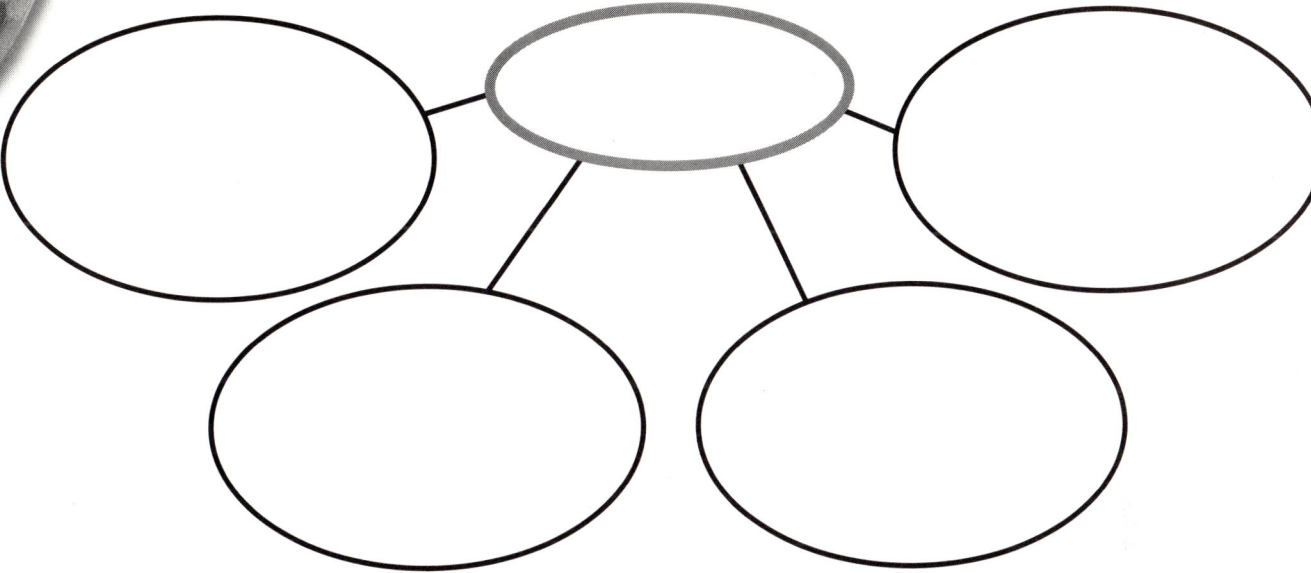

B. Writing Sentences Use the facts from the Web to write a list or short paragraph to analyze the civil rights leader you chose and why he or she was important.

_____
_____
_____
_____
_____

My Summary of the Lesson

Theme 3: Becoming Who We Are

Theme

A. Building a Word List Look at the pictures on page 128 of *ACCESS English*. Then list 4 words that come to mind when you look at them. Then tell what each word means.

1. _____
2. _____
3. _____
4. _____

B. Cause and Effect Think of two causes that have changed you or the way you think about the world. What change, or effect, did they create? Tell about the change by completing the Cause-Effect Organizer.

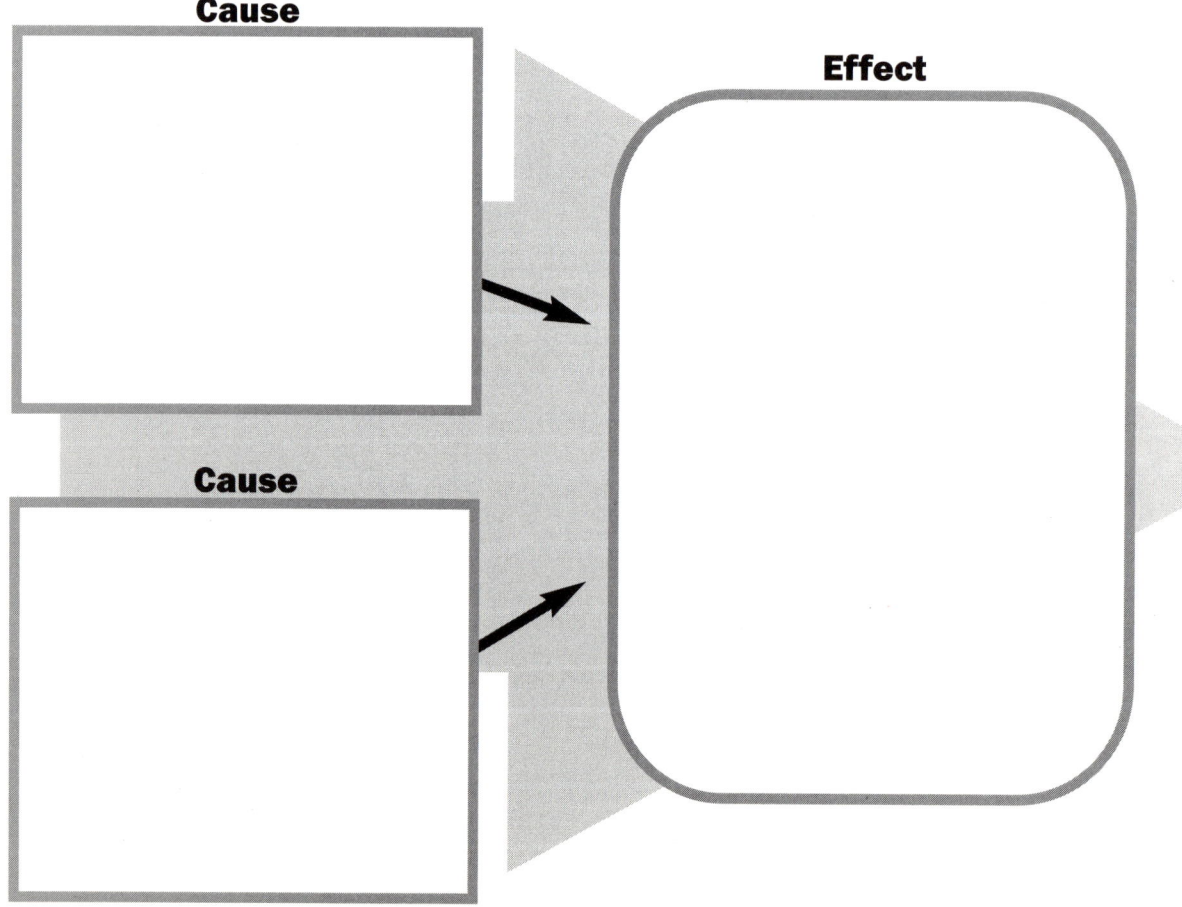

Name ______________________

FOR USE WITH PAGE 129

Literary Element

A. Definition Chart

Complete the Definition Chart below.

Word	Definition	Example Sentence
point of view		
autobiography		
experiences		

B. Point of View

Think about an argument you had with someone in your life. Try writing about it from your point of view. Then write it from the other person's point of view.

My point of view:

The other person's point of view:

Name

FOR USE WITH PAGES 130–133

Literature Connection

Showing Cause and Effect In *The Invisible Thread*, Yoshiko Uchida talks about the events that affected her life. In the Cause-Effect Organizers below, name 4 important experiences or memories from Yoshiko's childhood and their effects on her.

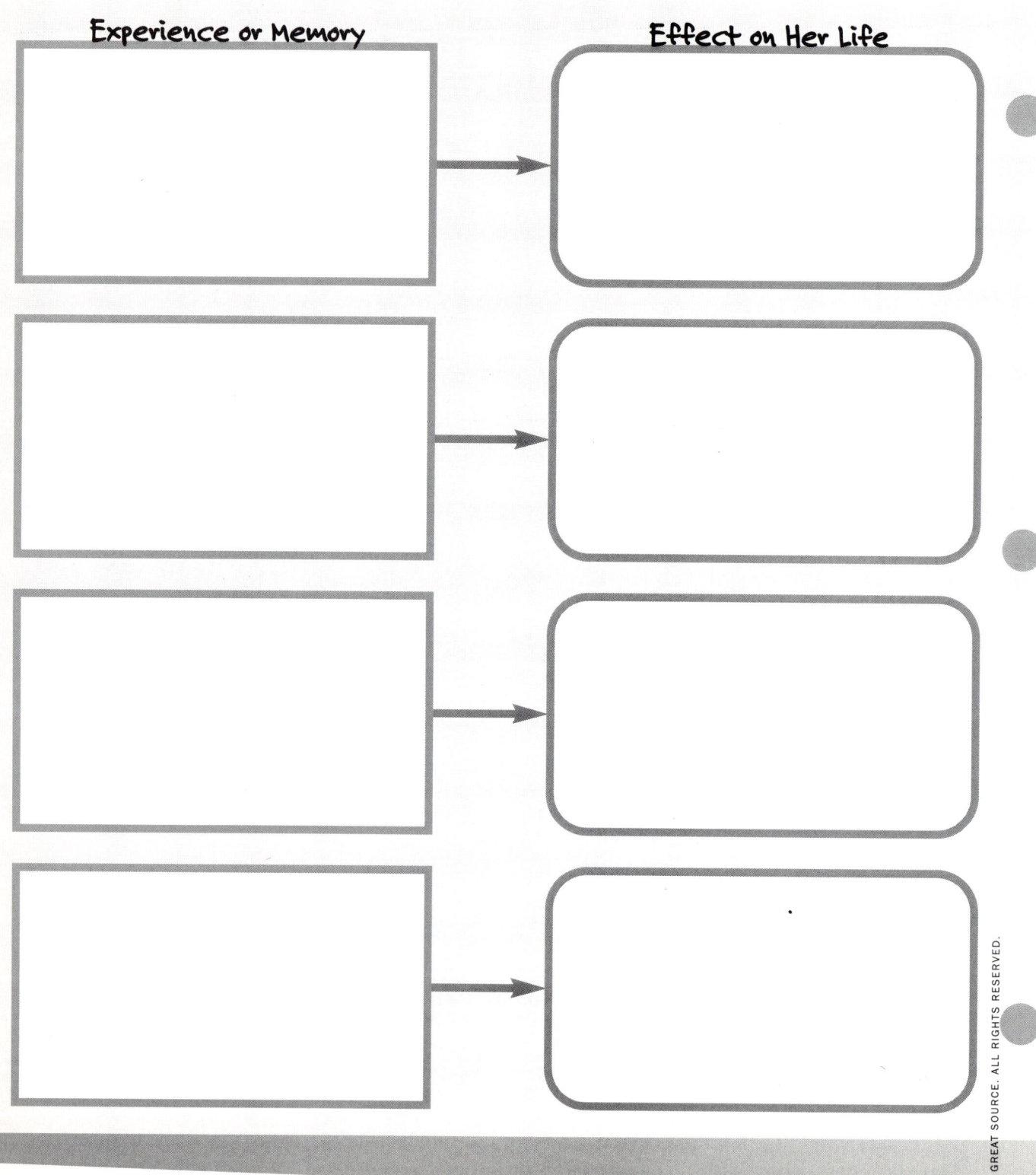

48 ACCESS ENGLISH

Name

Learn About Literature

Genre Choose two genres of literature you've read so far in *ACCESS English*. For each genre, name a title or work that you really enjoyed. Then tell what you like about it.

Genre:	What I Like About It:
Title:	

Genre:	What I Like About It:
Title:	

My Summary of the Lesson

Reading an Autobiography

My Word List

A. **Web** Complete the Web with the definitions of all 4 terms.

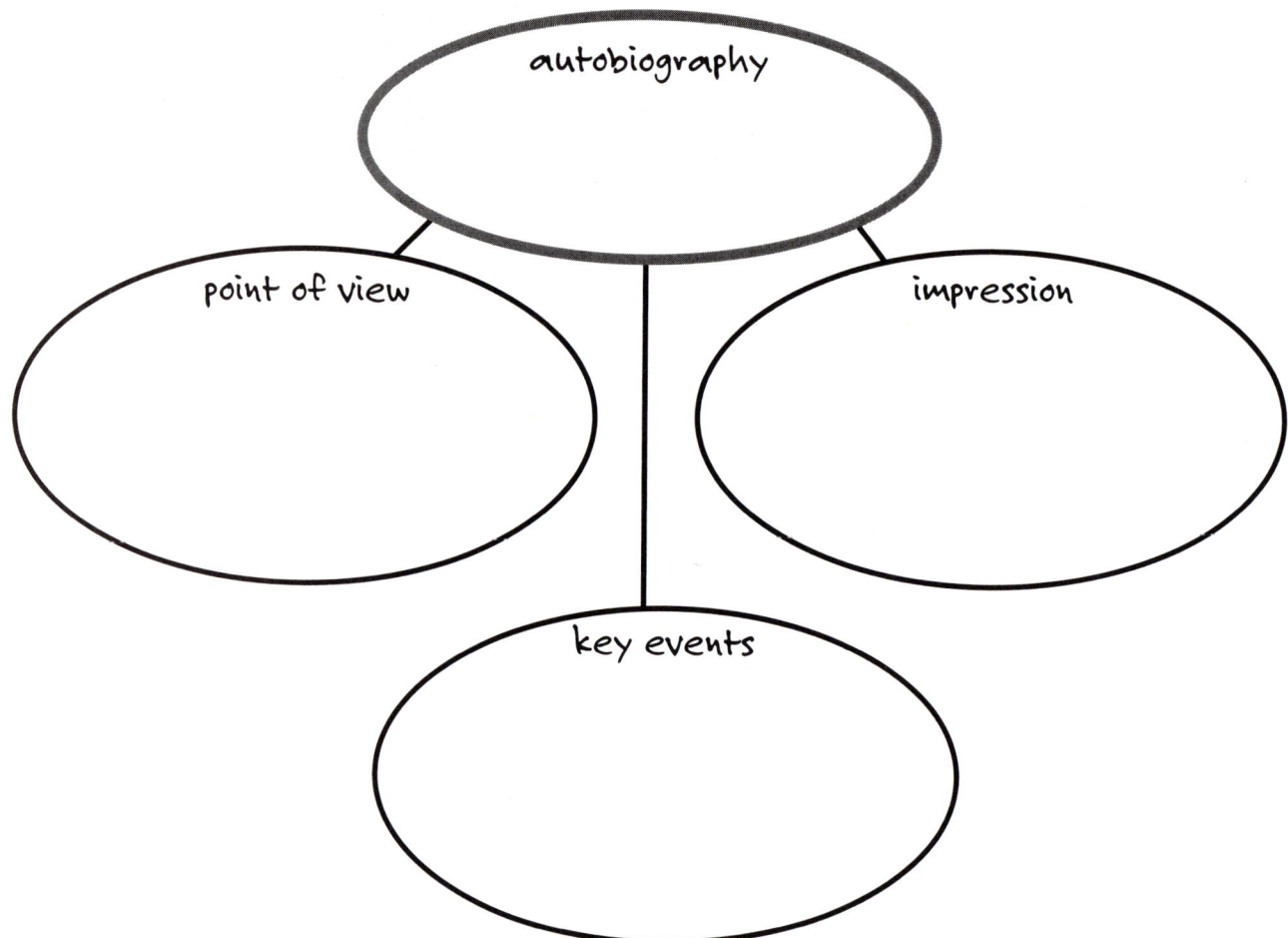

B. **Sentence Frame** Use the terms from your Web to complete this paragraph.

The Invisible Thread is an _____ by Yoshiko Uchida. Yoshiko offers an interesting _____ about identity. She feels out of place in the United States because she is Japanese. She had the _____ that Japan would feel more like home. Instead, she felt out of place there, too. Going to Japan was one of the _____ in Yoshiko's life. In Japan she realized she had her own special identity.

Name _____

FOR USE WITH PAGE 139

Lesson 9

Skill Building

A. Looking for Cause and Effect Think of 3 important events in your life (causes). Tell how they changed you (effects).

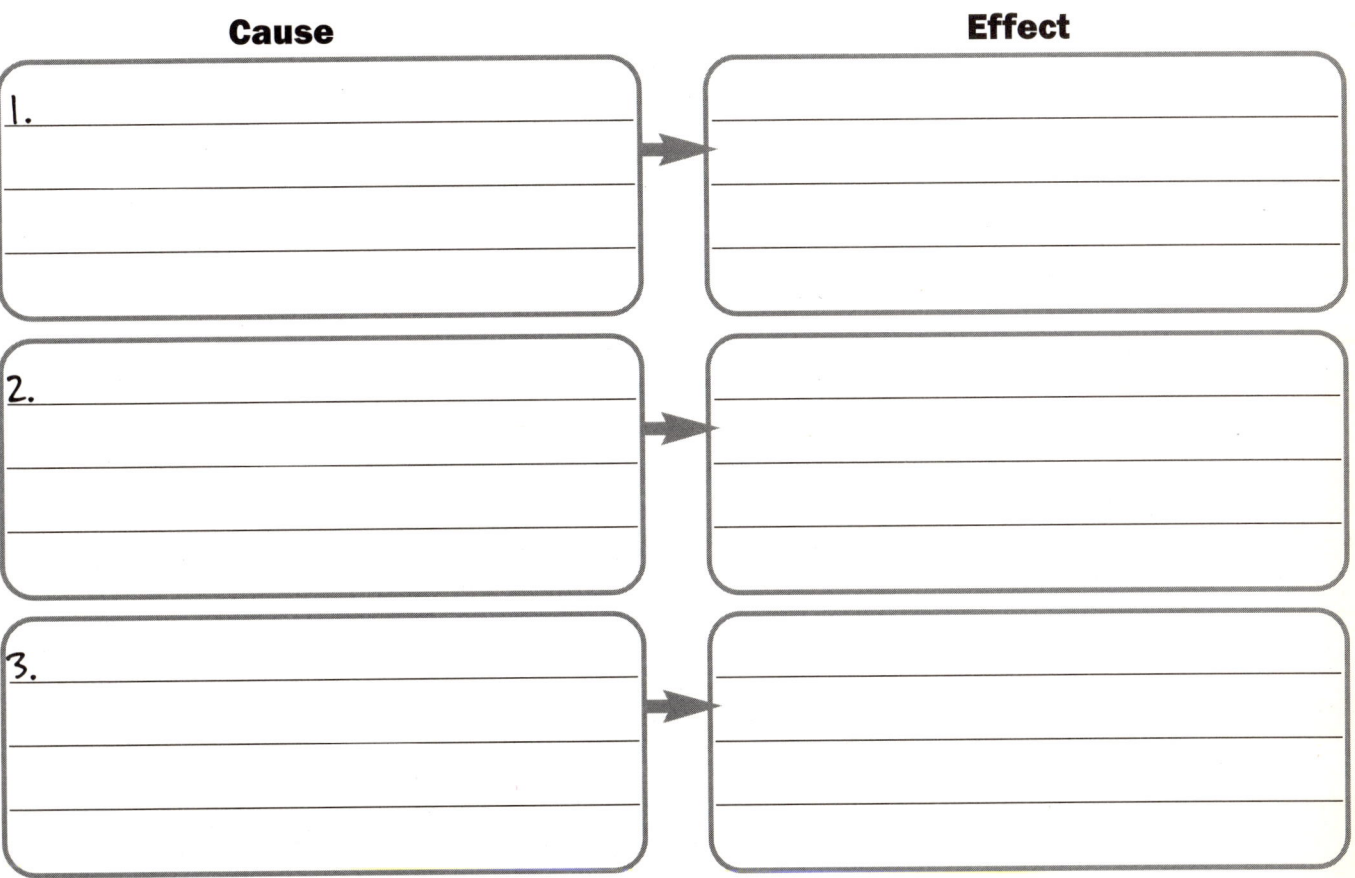

B. Writing Sentences Now write a short description or paragraph about one of the events you listed.

_____
_____
_____
_____
_____

LESSON 9 • READING AN AUTOBIOGRAPHY **51**

My Study Notes

A. Study Skill: Sequence Notes Use the sequence of the lesson to list the steps for reading an autobiography. Refer to pages 140–145 in *ACCESS English* if you need help.

1. Read for key events.

B. Key Details Use the Word Bank to fill in the blanks.

Anyone can write an autobiography. Everyone has a different story to tell and a different point of _____. A _____ event in your life can help make you who you are or form your personal _____. How you _____ these events and the _____ they make on you are important. Your losses can be just as interesting as your _____. You may not think your life is interesting enough to be a book, but if you tell about it in an interesting way, people will want to read it.

Word Bank
view
identity
achievements
major
perceive
impressions

Name _____

Lesson 9

FOR USE WITH PAGE 146

Showing What I Know

Synthesizing Review the Character Trait Web on page 146 in *ACCESS English*. Think of two character traits that describe you. Give two proofs for each.

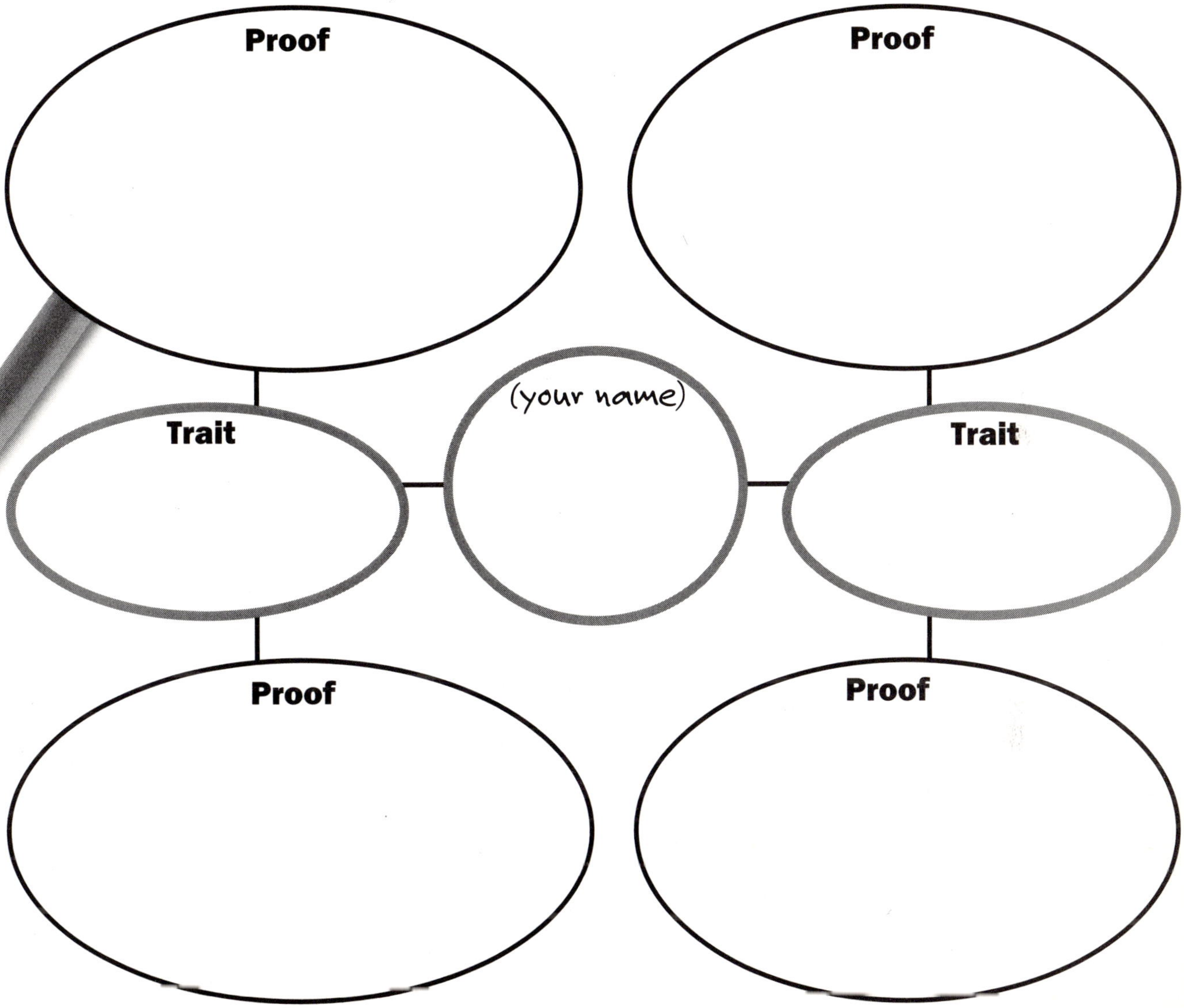

- Proof
- Proof
- Trait
- (your name)
- Trait
- Proof
- Proof

My Summary of the Lesson

LESSON 9 • READING AN AUTOBIOGRAPHY 53

Reading Graphics and Websites

My Word List

A. **Definition Chart** Complete the chart of Internet terms by writing their definitions. Use the glossary in *ACCESS English* if you need help.

Internet

Website

Graphics

Source

B. **Matching** Match each term with its example or definition.

Internet	•	• http://yahooligans.com
graphic	•	• World Wide Web
axes	•	• map of Uruguay
website	•	• lines in a bar graph that label information

Name

FOR USE WITH PAGE 151

Lesson **10**

Skill Building

A. Paraphrasing Use the Paraphrase Chart to explain the information in the pie chart at the bottom of page 150 of *ACCESS English*.

Subject	
My Paraphrase	
My Thoughts	

B. Writing Sentences Now look at the bar graph on page 151 of *ACCESS English*. Paraphrase the information in it in a few sentences.

_____
_____
_____
_____
_____

My Study Notes

A. Study Skill: Outlining the Lesson Outline the steps for reading graphics and websites. Use pages 152–157 of *ACCESS English* if you need help.

1. Looking at a Graphic
   a. Preview
   b.
2.
   a.
   b. Paraphrase
3.
   a.
   b. Evaluate the Source

B. Key Details Use the Word Bank to complete the sentences.

Word Bank
source
evaluate
reliable
symbols
expand

1. I could not find much about *Navajo population,* so I decided to _____ my search to *Navajo Indians.*
2. A good _____ for Internet research is a government website.
3. Make sure the Internet source you use is _____.
4. I always _____ a website I find so I know if it is reliable.
5. A key tells what the _____ on a graph represent.

Name

FOR USE WITH PAGE 158

Showing What I Know

Interpreting Find a graphic in a magazine or on the Internet. Read it carefully. Use the Summary Notes below to help you describe the graphic. Then use your Summary Notes to write a few sentences to interpret what the graphic means.

Title:

Main Point:

Important Facts:

1.

2.

3.

My Summary of the Lesson

Lesson 10

Writing an Expository Paragraph

My Word List

A. Definition Chart Complete the Definition Chart below. Use your glossary or page 162 of *ACCESS English* if you need help.

Word	Definition	Example Sentence
expository		
inform		
explain		
facts		
details		

B. Sentence Frames Use the words *details, inform, facts, explain,* and *expository* to complete the sentences.

Good _____ writing provides more than information. It also tells a story. The main purpose is to _____ the reader. Expository writing is based on reliable _____. There are many ways to make writing interesting. Give specific _____. If you _____ what it was like to be there, readers can connect with your writing.

Name

FOR USE WITH PAGE 163

Lesson 11

Skill Building

A. Using Time Order Put these events in time order by numbering them 1–5.

_____ On December 7, 1941, the Japanese military bombed Pearl Harbor.

_____ Japanese Americans were made to stay in the internment camps for a long time.

_____ Japanese Americans were seen as friends and Americans.

_____ Japanese Americans were now seen as enemies.

_____ In 1942, the U.S. president ordered Japanese Americans to move into internment camps.

B. Writing Sentences Use time order and write a short paragraph about Yoshiko's story. Remember to use signal words like *first*, *next*, *before*, *then*, and *after*. Reread pages 165–166 in *ACCESS English* if you need help remembering her story.

_____
_____
_____
_____
_____
_____
_____
_____
_____
_____

Name _____

FOR USE WITH PAGES 164–169

My Study Notes

A. Study Skill: Using Key Word or Topic Notes Explain each kind of order used in writing an expository paragraph.

Key Words or Topics	Notes
cause-effect order	
time order	

B. Sentence Frames Use the Word Bank to complete these sentences.

Our teacher asked us to write an _____ paragraph. The _____ of my paragraph was Japanese internment camps. I wanted to know what it was like to live in one, so I did _____ in the library. I found many _____ there, including a book by a man who was at Manzanar. The _____ of life in the camp were amazing. I hope nothing like that ever happens in the United States again!

Word Bank
details
expository
research
sources
subject

Name

Lesson 11

FOR USE WITH PAGE 170

Showing What I Know

A. **Identifying** Complete the Cause-Effect Organizer about why Japanese Americans were put into internment camps.

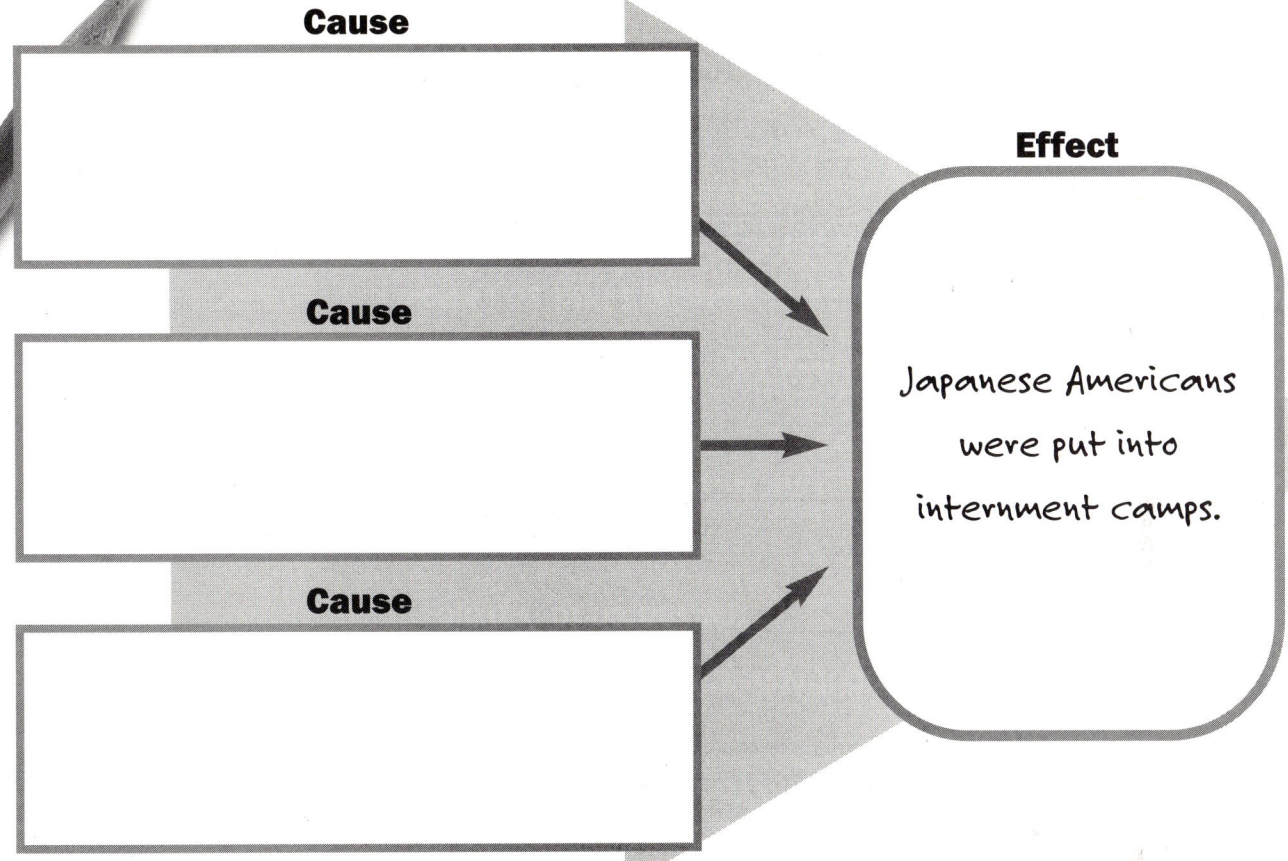

B. **Writing Sentences** Use the Cause-Effect Organizer to write a summary about why Japanese Americans were put into internment camps.

_____
_____
_____

My Summary of the Lesson

LESSON 11 • WRITING AN EXPOSITORY PARAGRAPH   **61**

Understanding Verbs

My Word List

A. Definition Chart Complete the Definition Chart below. In the last column, write a sentence with an example of the term.

Word	Definition	Example Sentence
subject		
verb		
predicate		

B. Labeling Sentence Parts Tell whether the underlined part of each sentence is the *subject*, *verb*, or *predicate*.

1. _____ My brother <u>woke up</u> at 7:00 A.M. because he was excited about his first day of karate class.

2. _____ <u>Amíl and I</u> went to a karate tournament last Saturday.

3. _____ Karate <u>gives</u> me a lot of confidence in myself.

4. _____ <u>Karate</u> is my favorite class.

5. _____ I <u>took my little sister to my next class</u>.

Lesson 12

FOR USE WITH PAGE 175

Skill Building

A. Revising Your Writing Write these passive voice sentences as active ones. Refer to the examples on page 175 of *ACCESS English*.

1. The test was given to us by the teacher.

2. My wallet was stolen by someone on the train.

3. Your funny comments were missed by everyone in class.

4. The queen was loved by all the people in the country.

5. The car was driven by my older cousin, Benny.

B. Writing Sentences Now write 5 sentences of your own in active voice. Write about some of the characters you have read about in *ACCESS English*.

1.

2.

3.

4.

5.

LESSON 12 • UNDERSTANDING VERBS

Name

My Study Notes

FOR USE WITH PAGES 176–181

A. Study Skill: Understanding Verbs Write a sentence with an example of each type of verb. Underline your example.

Verb	Example
action verb	
linking verb	
helping verb	

B. Key Details Tell whether the verb in each sentence is an action verb, a linking verb, or a helping verb.

1. John and Rosa *danced* all night. _____
2. Suzanna *looks* pretty in her new sweater. _____
3. Otaka *will* help her sister with her homework. _____
4. Our dog always *barks* at the neighbor's cat. _____
5. I *am* worried about my history test. _____
6. The night air *feels* cool. _____
7. I *love* fajitas. _____

Name

FOR USE WITH PAGE 182

Showing What I Know

A. Identifying Complete the Verb Chart with the correct tense of each verb.

Present Tense	Past Tense	Future Tense
laugh		
buy		
fall		
smile		
is		
learn		
try		
do		
become		
feel		

B. Writing Sentences Write a sentence using an action verb in a tense you choose. Make sure your subject and verb agree.

Sentence: _____
_____
_____

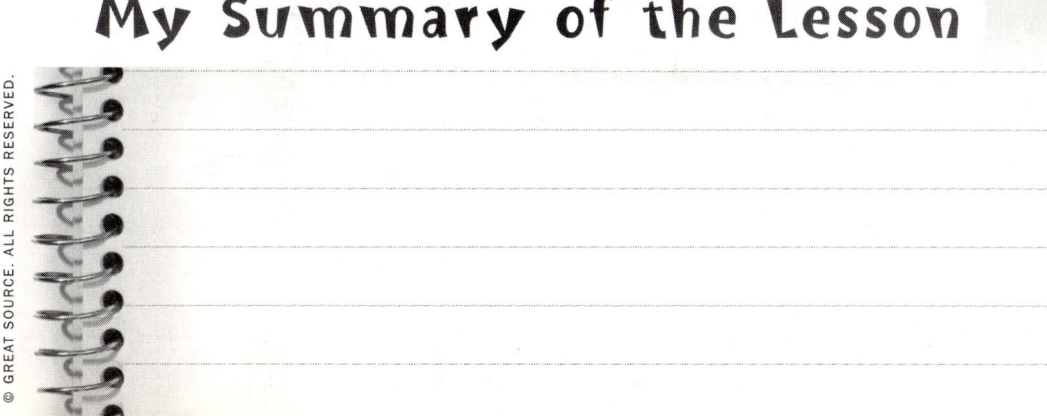

My Summary of the Lesson

LESSON 12 • UNDERSTANDING VERBS

Theme 4: Life Journeys

Theme

A. Writing Sentences Look at the pictures on page 184 of *ACCESS English*. How do you think these people feel as they begin their journeys? Choose a person and write a few sentences about what he or she might be thinking.

_____
_____
_____
_____
_____
_____
_____

B. Brainstorm Use the Web below to brainstorm a list of words about journeys.

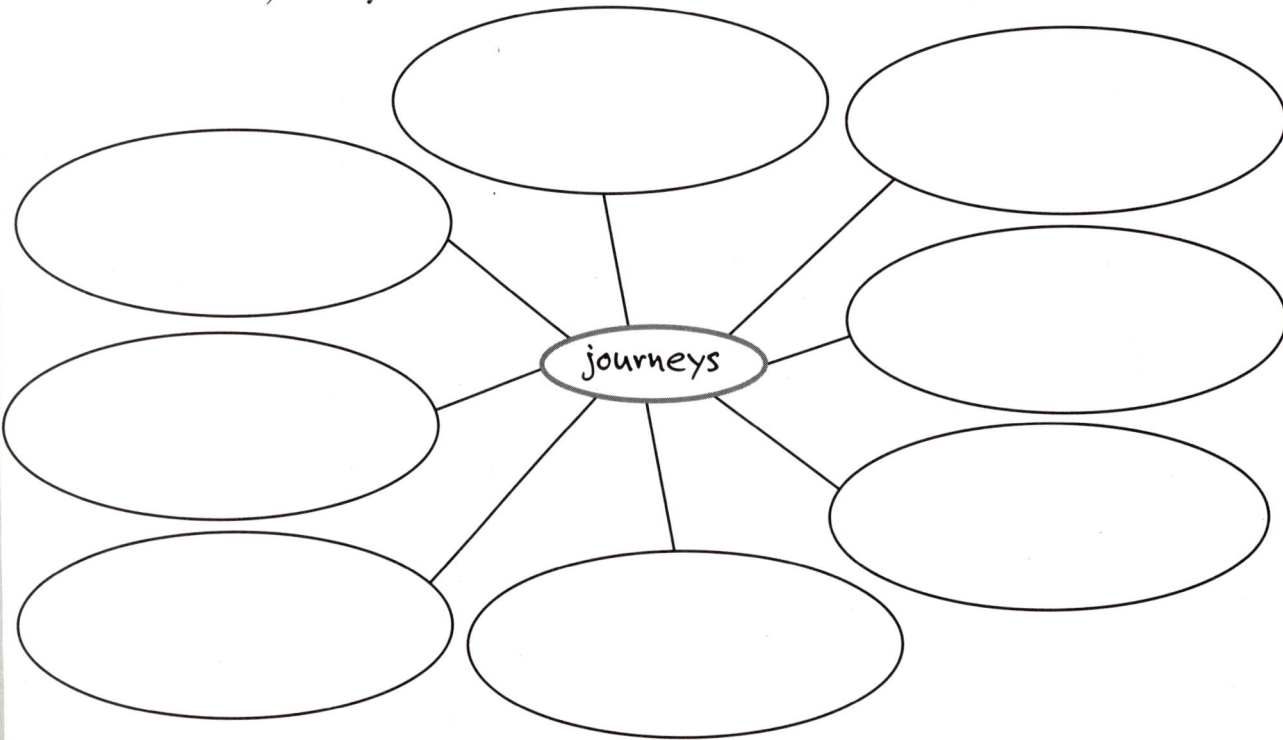

Name ______________________________

FOR USE WITH PAGE 185

Literary Element

A. Definition Chart

Complete the Definition Chart below.

Word	Definition	Example Sentence
fact		
opinion		

B. Fact or Opinion

Write whether the following sentences are *fact* or *opinion.*

1. ____________ Harriet Tubman helped slaves escape to freedom.
2. ____________ The journey on the Underground Railroad was long and difficult.
3. ____________ If the runaways were caught, they would be sold back to Southern slave owners.
4. ____________ Harriet Tubman was never caught, and she never lost a slave.
5. ____________ It takes a brave person to risk his or her life for others.

Name _____

FOR USE WITH PAGES 186–189

Literature Connection

Supporting Your Opinion Give an opinion about Harriet Tubman or the Underground Railroad. Complete the Web with 3 facts to support your opinion.

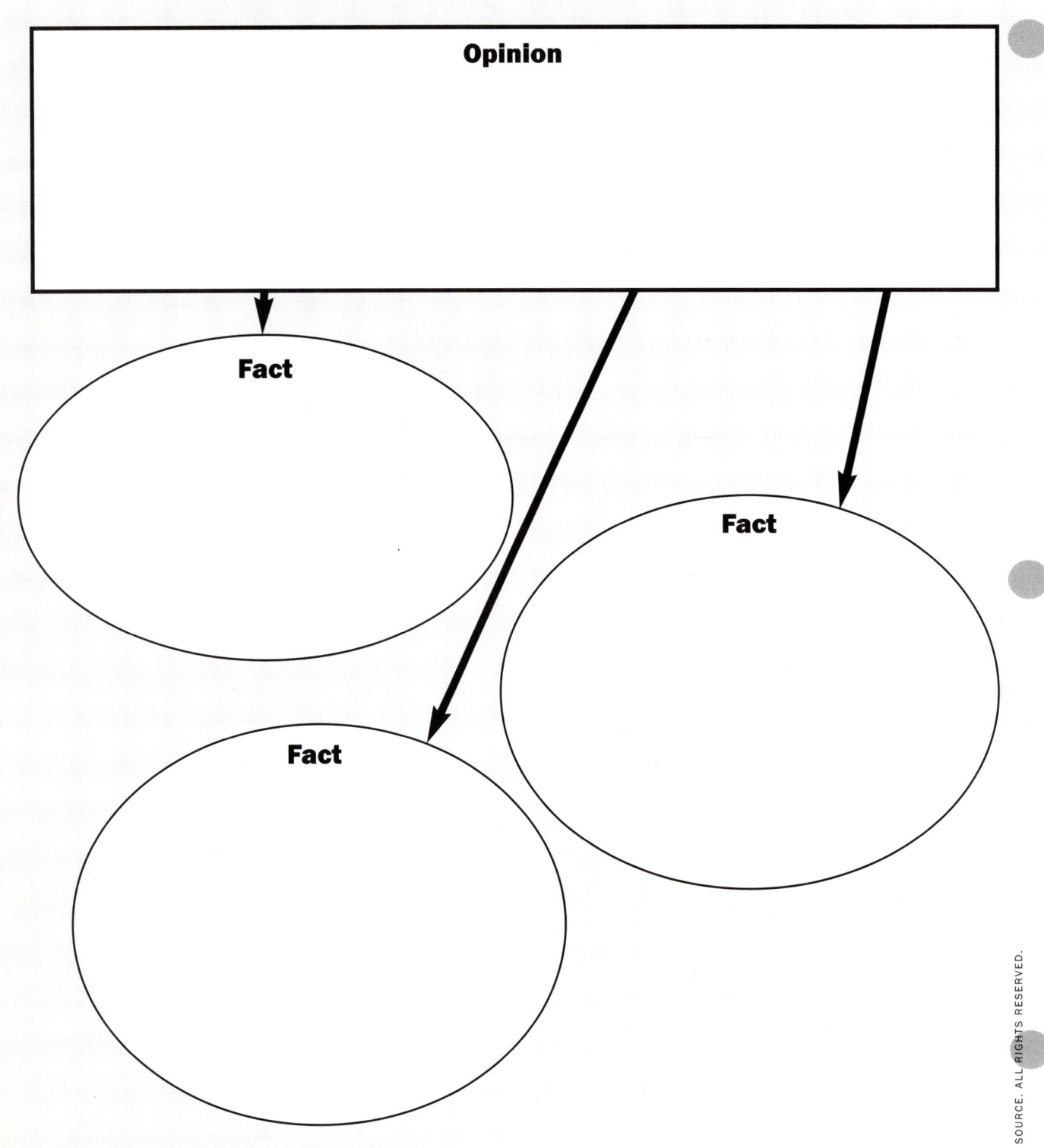

68 ACCESS ENGLISH

Name _____

Theme 4

FOR USE WITH PAGE 190

Learn About Literature

Dialogue Draw a picture of Harriet Tubman talking to slaves about the Underground Railroad. Then write some dialogue for what they might be talking about.

My Summary of the Lesson

Reading Textbooks

My Word List

A. Definition Chart Complete the Definition Chart below. Use the glossary in *ACCESS English* if you need help.

Word	Definition	Example Sentence
note-taking		
headings		
table of contents		
chapter		

B. Sentence Frames Use words from the Definition Chart to fill in the blanks.

The first step in good _____ involves knowing what to look at first. Before you begin, look at the _____ to see what's in the book. Look for the title of the _____ you will be reading. Sometimes the sections of the textbook will be divided into smaller sections called _____.

Lesson 13

Name

FOR USE WITH PAGE 195

Skill Building

A. Previewing Preview the lesson that begins on page 192 of *ACCESS English*. Then fill in the Preview Organizer.

Title:
Big Idea:
Key Concepts:
Boldface Words:

B. Writing Sentences Use the Preview Organizer to write a few sentences about what you may learn from this lesson.

_____
_____
_____
_____
_____

LESSON 13 • READING TEXTBOOKS 71

Name _____

FOR USE WITH PAGES 196–201

My Study Notes

A. **Study Skill: Outlining the Lesson** Use the lesson headings to complete the study outline below.

Reading Textbooks
1. Use the Reading Process
    a.
    b.
    c.
2. Ways of Taking Notes
    a.
    b.
    c.

B. **Key Details** Use the Word Bank to answer these questions about textbooks.

1. Where in the book can you find definitions for words?

_____

2. Where would you look if you wanted to know all the pages about nouns?

_____

3. What is the term used when a word appears darker than the other words in the text?

_____

4. What is another word for one type of picture in your textbook?

_____

5. What do you call the writing under the pictures in your textbook?

_____

Word Bank
captions
glossary
index
photos
boldface

72 ACCESS ENGLISH

Name _____

FOR USE WITH PAGE 202

Lesson **13**

Showing What I Know

A. Comparing and Contrasting Use a Venn Diagram to compare and contrast two kinds of note-taking you learned about in this lesson.

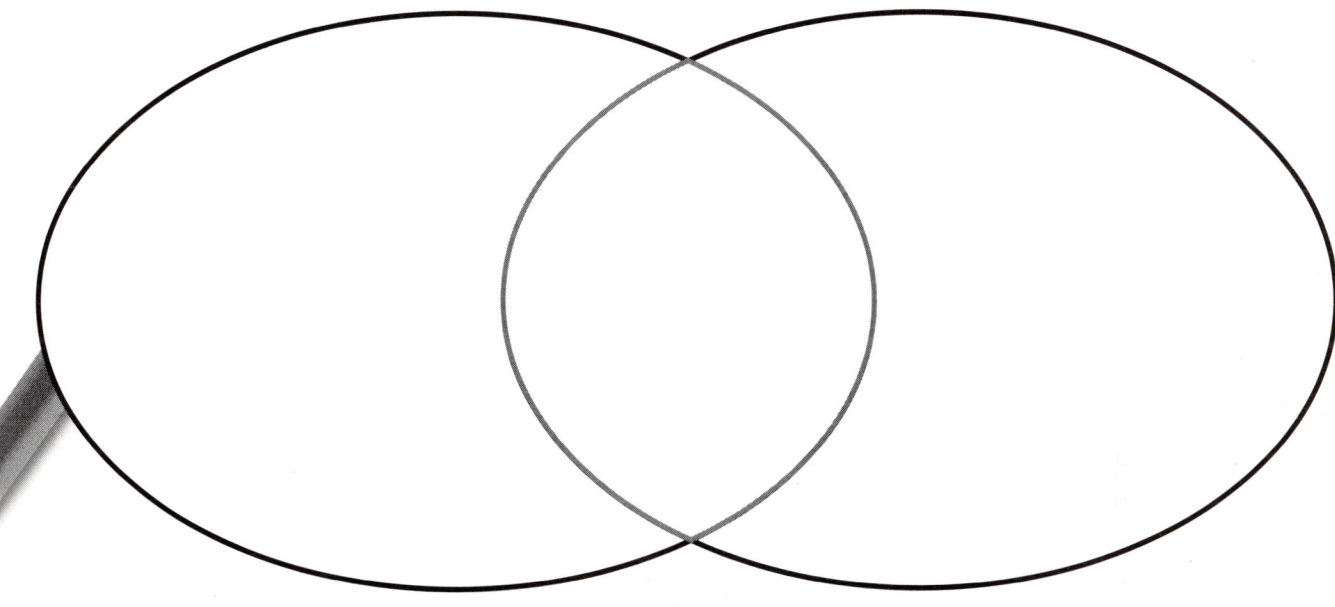

B. Writing Sentences Which form of note-taking would be more useful for reading this lesson? Give reasons for your answer.

_____
_____
_____
_____
_____

My Summary of the Lesson

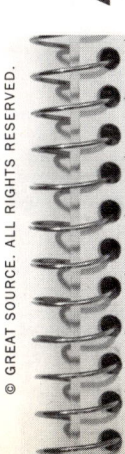

LESSON 13 • READING TEXTBOOKS   73

Reading Tests

My Word List

A. Definition Chart Use the Key Concepts on page 206 of *ACCESS English* to complete the Definition Chart below.

Word	Definition
fact or recall questions	
inference questions	
skimming	

B. Answering Questions Use the words from the Definition Chart to help answer these questions.

1. What type of questions ask you to put together facts to make a judgment?

2. What type of questions ask you to remember a detail about what you read?

3. What is the best way to quickly find out what the text is about?

Name _____

Lesson 14

FOR USE WITH PAGE 207

Skill Building

Drawing Conclusions From 1850 to 1863, people in the United States argued bitterly over slavery. Study the timeline below.

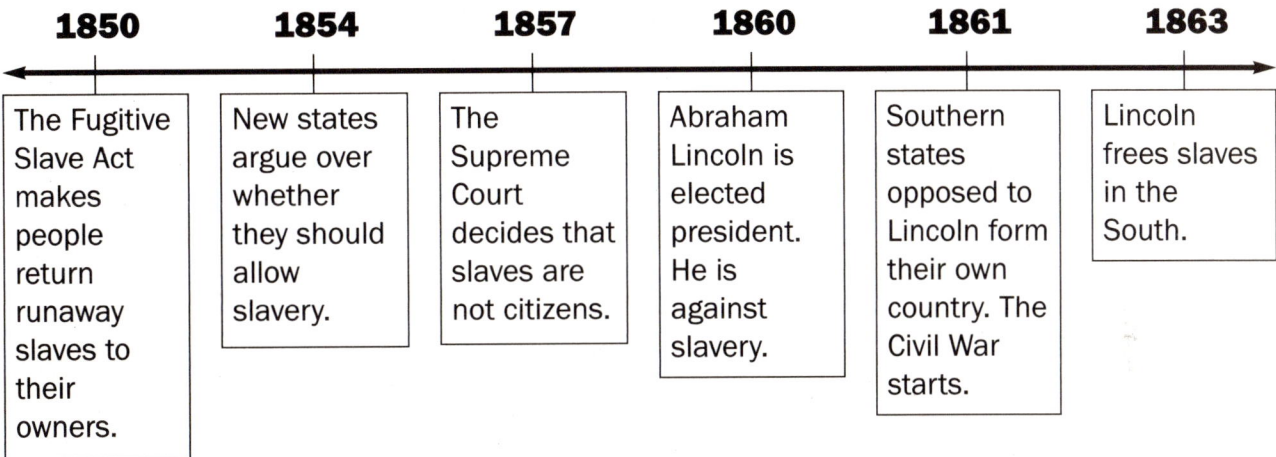

What two conclusions can you draw from the timeline above? Write sentences stating your conclusions about slavery in the United States.

_____
_____
_____
_____
_____
_____
_____
_____
_____

My Study Notes

A. **Study Skill: Outlining the Lesson** Use pages 208–213 of *ACCESS English* to help you complete the study outline below.

1. Prepare for the Test
   a.
   b.
   c.
   d.
2. Skim for Fact Questions
3. Read Closely for Inference Questions
4. Three Steps for Essay Questions
   a.
   b.
   c.

B. **Key Details** Use the Word Bank to complete these sentences.

1. Science is always a _____ for me, so I have to study hard.
2. The words *sink* and *drink* _____.
3. Make sure you are prepared for any _____ tests.
4. My favorite _____ in the book is the part about freedom for all people.
5. On an essay test, we'll be asked to write an _____ paragraph.
6. My math teacher said our final exam will cover all the _____ we learned this semester.

Word Bank
rhyme
upcoming
challenge
material
passage
expository

Name _____

Lesson 14

FOR USE WITH PAGE 214

Showing What I Know

Evaluating Go back to *Harriet Tubman: Conductor on the Underground Railroad* on pages 186–189 in *ACCESS English*. Use the Evaluation Chart below to organize your ideas about the Underground Railroad.

Subject: Underground Railroad		
Detail	**Detail**	**Detail**

My Evaluation:

My Summary of the Lesson

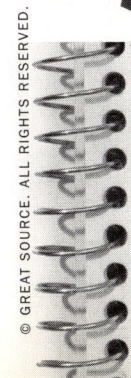

LESSON 14 • READING TESTS   77

Writing Reports

My Word List

A. **Magnet Summary** Complete the Magnet Summary about research by stating what happens during each step.

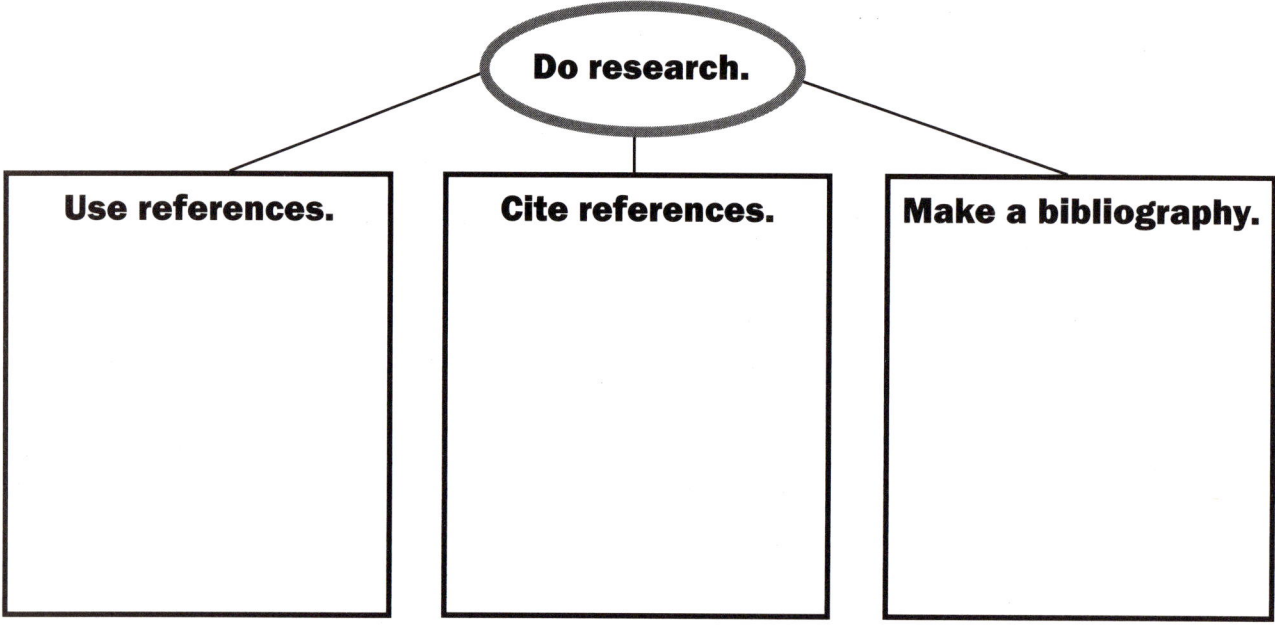

B. **Matching** Match the terms with their examples. Then find one reference source about the Great Migration. This can be from the library or the Internet. Cite the source in the space below.

Use references	• Find information about the Great Migration, 1910–1930.
Make a bibliography/ Cite references	• encyclopedias, Internet, books from the library
Do research	• 1. Lawrence, Jacob. *The Great Migration: An American Story.* New York: HarperTrophy, 1995. 2. http://www.pbs.org/wnet/aaworld/reference/articles/great_migration.html

My Source: _____

Name _____

FOR USE WITH PAGE 219

Lesson 15

Skill Building

A. **Narrowing a Topic**   Choose a topic you would like to write a paper about. Write the topic in the center of the Web. Write 4 ideas about that topic in the other spaces.

B. **Writing Questions**   Now write 5 questions about your topic asking *Who* or *What? When? Where? Why? How?*

1. Who or what? _____

_____

2. When? _____

_____

3. Where? _____

_____

4. Why? _____

_____

5. How? _____

_____

LESSON 15 • WRITING REPORTS   79

Name _____

FOR USE WITH PAGES 220–225

My Study Notes

A. Study Skill: Explaining Steps Use pages 220–225 in *ACCESS English* to help you complete the steps for writing a report. Tell what happens during each step.

1. Getting Started _____
   a. _____
   b. _____
   c. _____

2. Writing the First Draft _____
   a. _____
   b. _____
   c. _____

3. Finishing Your Report _____
   a. _____
   b. _____
   c. _____

B. Key Details Use the Word Bank to complete these sentences.

1. Before writing your paper, make an _____ of the things you will write about.

2. _____ information you find in books instead of copying exactly what they say.

3. Research is easier if you _____ some ideas first.

4. A paper should have clear _____, with a beginning, a middle, and an ending.

Word Bank
paraphrase
organization
brainstorm
outline

80 ACCESS ENGLISH

Name _____

Lesson 15

FOR USE WITH PAGE 226

Showing What I Know

Synthesizing   Make a Gathering Grid using the topic you chose on page 79. Answer 3 of the questions you wrote on that page. You will need to find two reference sources to do so. Cite them on your grid. Follow the example on page 226 in *ACCESS English*.

Subject:	Source 1:	Source 2:
Question 1:	Answer:	Answer:
Question 2:	Answer:	Answer:
My Synthesis:		

My Summary of the Lesson

LESSON 15 • WRITING REPORTS   81

More About Verbs

My Word List

A. Verb Examples Give examples of each kind of verb below. Use page 230 of *ACCESS English* if you need help.

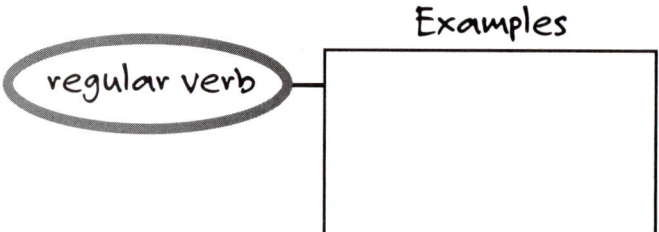

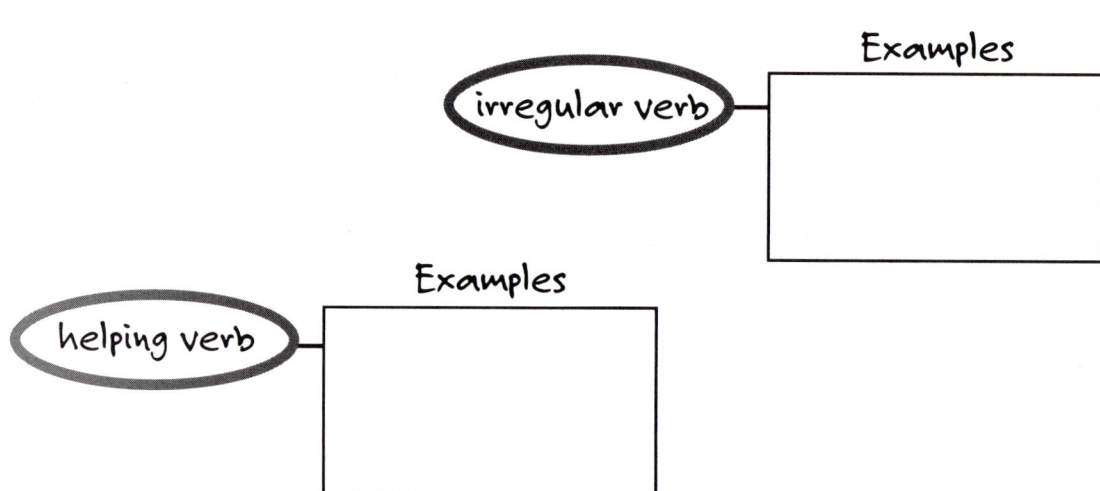

B. Labeling Sentence Parts Tell whether the underlined verb is an action verb, linking verb, or helping verb.

1. _____ The first people to play jazz <u>were</u> black musicians in New Orleans in the early 20th century.

2. _____ The Harlem Renaissance <u>began</u> in the 1920s.

3. _____ Jazz music <u>became</u> popular during the Harlem Renaissance.

4. _____ Duke Ellington <u>had</u> written over 1,000 songs before he died.

5. _____ Louis Armstrong <u>was</u> famous for playing the trumpet.

Name

FOR USE WITH PAGE 231

Lesson 16

Skill Building

A. Revising: Using Strong, Vivid Verbs Preview Lesson 16 in *ACCESS English*. Write down 5 vivid verbs that you see in the pictures.

1. _____
2. _____
3. _____
4. _____
5. _____

B. Writing Sentences Write 5 sentences about a fictional character or a real person you have read about. What was the person's life journey like? Use strong verbs.

1. _____
_____
2. _____
_____
3. _____
_____
4. _____
_____
5. _____
_____

LESSON 16 • MORE ABOUT VERBS

Name _____

FOR USE WITH PAGES 232–237

My Study Notes

A. Study Skill: Using a Verb Chart Complete the Verb Chart with the correct forms of each verb. For the present participle and past particle verbs, include a helping verb. Refer to page 237 in *ACCESS English*.

Present	Present Participle	Past	Past Participle
bounce			
stand			
smile			
break			
try			
swim			
bring			
drop			
fall			
cut			

B. Key Details Use the Word Bank to complete these sentences.

1. Add the _____ ed to make a regular verb past tense.
2. The present _____ form of *sigh* is *sighing*.
3. A verb is _____ when the action is done to the subject.
4. A verb is _____ if the subject is doing the action.
5. There are 4 _____ verb parts.

Word Bank
principal
participle
suffix
passive
active

84 ACCESS ENGLISH

Lesson 16

Name _____

FOR USE WITH PAGE 238

Showing What I Know

A. Demonstrating Complete the Verb Chart using 3 action verbs and 3 helping verbs. Demonstrate how each is used in a sentence.

Action Verbs	Example Sentences
1.	
2.	
3.	
Helping Verbs	**Example Sentences**
1.	
2.	
3.	

B. Picture It Change the sentences below to make the verbs present participle verbs.

Enrique rescued his sister.
_____

Kelli lives near me.
_____

Paolo played soccer today.
_____

My Summary of the Lesson

LESSON 16 • MORE ABOUT VERBS 85

Theme 5: Our Place

Theme

A. **Picture It** The people in the pictures on page 240 of *ACCESS English* are at home in their community. List 10 words that describe your community. Draw a picture of it and label it with the words from the list.

1. _____
2. _____
3. _____
4. _____
5. _____
6. _____
7. _____
8. _____
9. _____
10. _____

B. **Writing Sentences** Do you have a place you call your own? Write a few sentences about it.

_____
_____
_____
_____
_____
_____
_____

Name

Theme 5

FOR USE WITH PAGE 241

Literary Element

A. **Definition Chart** Use page 241 in *ACCESS English* to help you complete the Definition Chart below.

Word	Definition	Example Sentence
theme		
clues		
statement		

B. **K-W-L Chart** The theme of this lesson is "our place." What do you think this means? As you read the lesson, complete the K-W-L Chart below for this theme. Use the example on page 241 as a model.

What I Know	What I Want to Know	What I Learned

Name

FOR USE WITH PAGES 242–251

Literature Connection

Supporting an Opinion In "The Circuit," Panchito and his family move many times. What place does Panchito have to call his own? Write your answer in the bottom oval of the Web. Support your answer with 3 details or opinions.

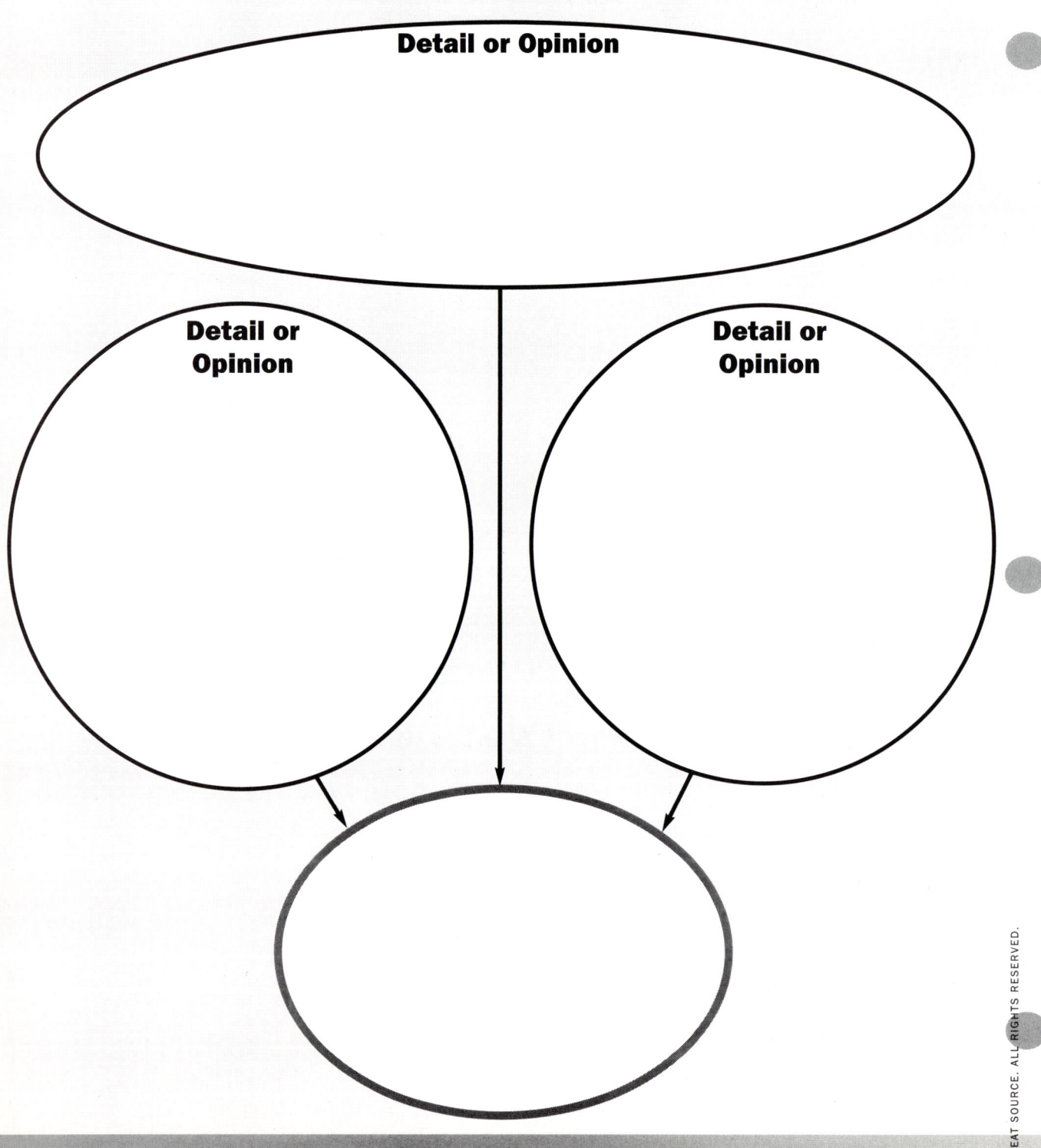

Name _____

Theme 5

FOR USE WITH PAGE 252

Learn About Literature

Irony Give one example of irony in "The Circuit." Write the example below. Then tell why it is ironic.

_____
_____
_____
_____
_____
_____
_____
_____
_____
_____
_____
_____
_____
_____
_____
_____
_____

My Summary of the Lesson

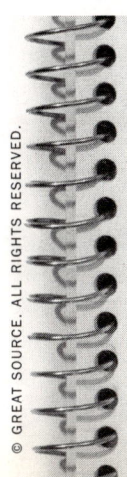

Reading a Story

My Word List

A. Definition Chart Use the Key Concepts on page 256 of *ACCESS English* to complete the Definition Chart below.

Word	Definition
genre	
fiction	
realistic fiction	

B. Giving Examples Give specific examples of the genres below using literature you heard about or read in *ACCESS English*.

1. fiction:

2. nonfiction:

3. poetry:

Skill Building

A. **Making Inferences** Read the sentences below. Make inferences about what they say.

1. My dad served the chicken. Some of it landed on the table. My dad apologized before putting it onto Alice's plate.

   Inference: _____

2. It was dark outside when I got home. My mother was waiting in the living room, and the look on her face said it all.

   Inference: _____

3. We just got our math tests back, so I probably will not be allowed to go to the party this weekend.

   Inference: _____

4. I was looking everywhere for my new shirt until I remembered my sister was going out that night.

   Inference: _____

5. A dog wandered by, dragging its leash. A few minutes later, a man walked by and looked around.

   Inference: _____

B. **Writing Sentences** Write a few sentences that let a reader infer that it is a hot day.

_____
_____
_____
_____

Name _____

FOR USE WITH PAGES 258–263

My Study Notes

A. Study Skill: Key Word or Topic Notes Complete the Key Word or Topic Notes for this lesson. Explain what each part of a story is.

Key Words or Topics	Notes
setting	
characters	
plot	
theme	

B. Key Details Use the Word Bank to complete these sentences.

1. The _____ of the story is when Doug finally meets his father.
2. Fictional stories are usually about _____ characters.
3. The _____ between Yao and Mia began when Yao told everyone Mia's secret.
4. The _____ of the story was the little boy who told the story as an adult.
5. I was not satisfied with the _____ of that story, even though everyone was happy in the end.

Word Bank
imaginary
conflict
climax
narrator
resolution

92 ACCESS ENGLISH

Name _____

Lesson 17

FOR USE WITH PAGE 264

Showing What I Know

Synthesizing Complete the Fiction Organizer below for a story you know or have heard.

Characters

Setting

Plot

Title

Theme

My Summary of the Lesson

LESSON 17 • READING A STORY   93

Writing a Narrative Paragraph

My Word List

A. Definition Chart Use the glossary to complete the Definition Chart below.

Word	Definition
narrative	
chronological order	
experience	
draft	
details	

B. Sentence Frames Use the words above in the Definition Chart to complete this paragraph.

A _____ paragraph can be interesting when written about an _____ that really happened to you. You can then provide vivid _____ because you are writing about a real event. Just remember when writing your first _____ to describe the event clearly. A good way to do this is to tell what happened in _____. Telling events in the order in which they happened gives your paragraph a clear beginning, middle, and end.

Skill Building

Writing with Voice Write 1–2 sentences about each of these topics. Use your own voice. Let your feelings show and make sure your writing sounds like you. Follow the 3 tips on page 269 of *ACCESS English*.

1. Your favorite musician:

2. Something you enjoy doing:

3. Something you think is unfair:

4. What you would do if you won a million dollars:

5. Someone you like or admire:

My Study Notes

A. Study Skill: Outlining the Lesson Complete the outline for writing a narrative paragraph. Tell what you do in each step. Use pages 270–275 of *ACCESS English* if you need help.

1. Starting Your Paragraph
   a. _____
   b. _____
2. Writing Your Paragraph
   a. _____
   b. _____
3. Revising and Editing Your Paragraph
   a. _____
   b. _____
   c. _____
   d. _____

B. Key Details Use the Word Bank to complete the sentences.

1. Sentence _____ means connecting sentences so that there is a smooth flow from one idea to the next.
2. _____ experiences from your life make good subjects for writing.
3. To write a good narrative paragraph, tell what happened and make sure your ideas flow _____.
4. Be _____ about what you write, leaving out details that are not important to the story.

Word Bank
memorable
selective
fluency
smoothly

Name _____

Lesson 18

FOR USE WITH PAGE 276

Showing What I Know

Describing Complete the 5 W's and H Organizer with a personal experience from your life.

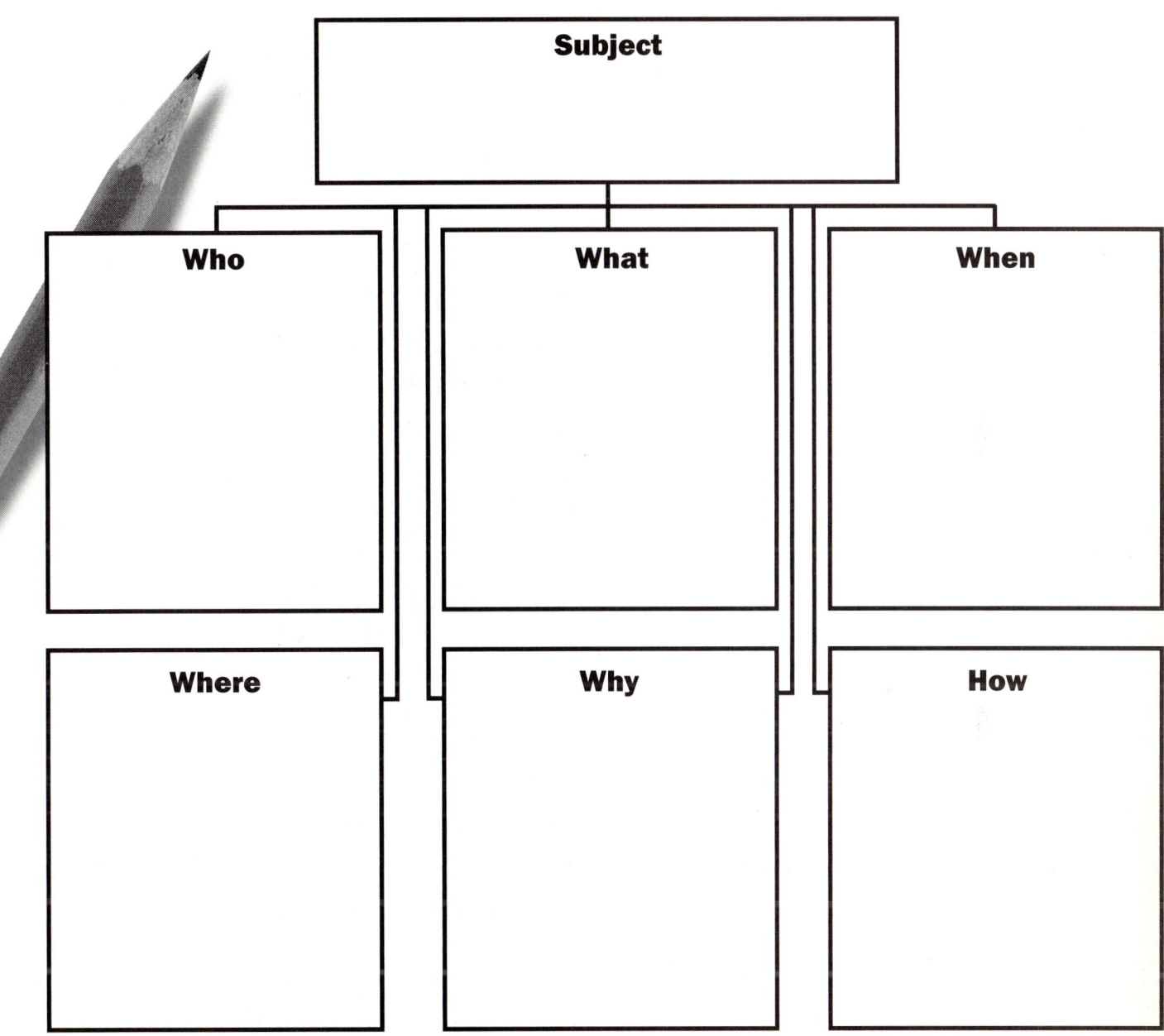

My Summary of the Lesson

_____
_____
_____
_____
_____

LESSON 18 • WRITING A NARRATIVE PARAGRAPH   97

Writing a Story

My Word List

A. Summary Chart Complete the chart below with the definitions for the terms.

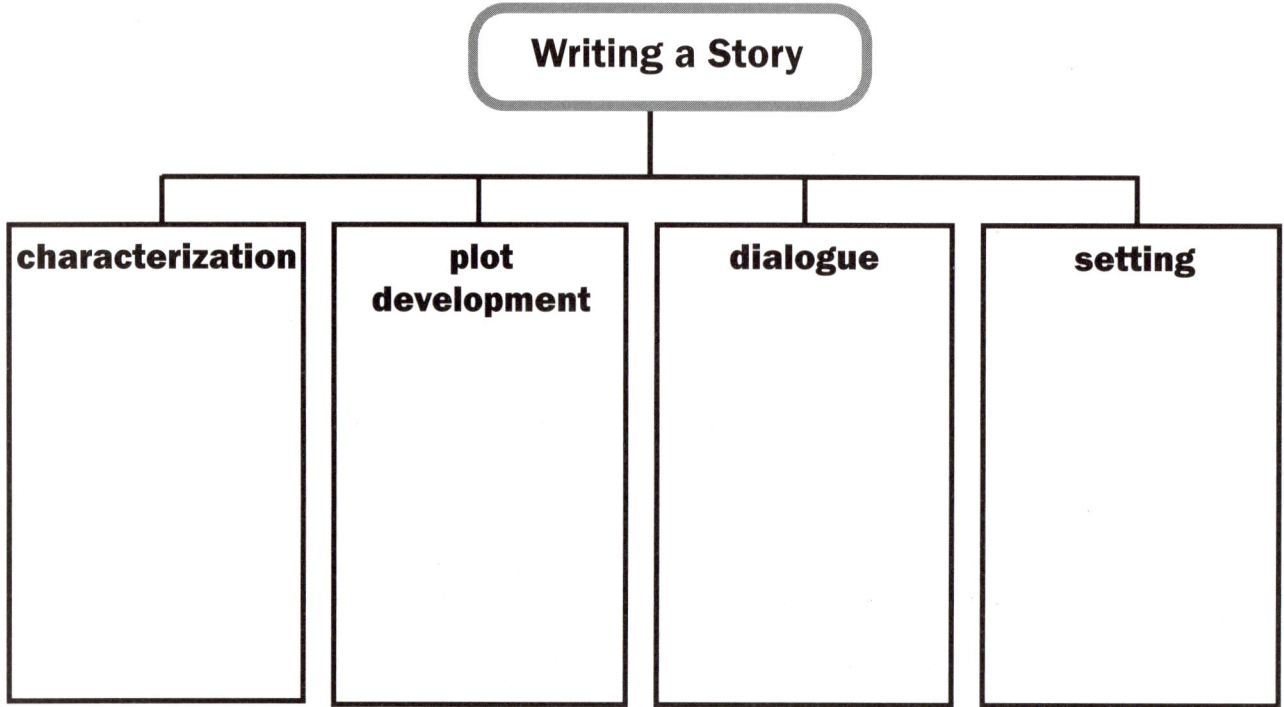

B. Matching Match each term with its example.

plot development	•	• The boy was small and quiet. He smiled shyly when spoken to.
characterization	•	• The town he grew up in was a dusty, deserted stop along a highway.
setting	•	• "Something is wrong," I said.
dialogue	•	• Smoke drifted from the car and then stopped. The car would not start again. We were stuck.

Lesson 19

FOR USE WITH PAGE 281

Name

Skill Building

A. Writing Dialogue Rewrite the sentences below so that the dialogue has correct punctuation. Use page 281 in *ACCESS English* to help you.

1. Manuela opened the door just as Kim said we shouldn't do this, guys.

2. She asked me do you know where we're going.

3. The ball came speeding toward my head, and she yelled look out.

4. She said good morning.

5. That sounds like a great idea I said.

B. Creating a Dialogue Now write a short dialogue between two people in which one person asks the other a question. Be sure to use correct punctuation.

LESSON 19 • WRITING A STORY 99

My Study Notes

A. Study Skill: Outlining the Lesson Complete the outline for writing a story. Use pages 282–287 in *ACCESS English* if you need help.

1. Developing Parts of a Story
    a. The Plot
    b.
    c.
2. Writing Your Story
    a. Plan Your Story
    b.
    c.
    d.
    e.

B. Key Details Use the Word Bank to complete these sentences.

1. The _____ is a girl who runs away from home, and the story is about her experiences.
2. Some of the _____ are the people she meets during her travels.
3. The _____ in the story is how the girl struggles to face her problems.
4. Intelligence and stubbornness are two _____ that define her.
5. Her tough _____ helps her survive.

Word Bank
personality
characteristics
conflict
minor characters
main character

Name _____

Lesson **19**

FOR USE WITH PAGE 288

Showing What I Know

A. Explaining Use the Story String to put together a story you want to tell. Remember the 3 main elements of a story that you learned about: plot development, setting, and characters.

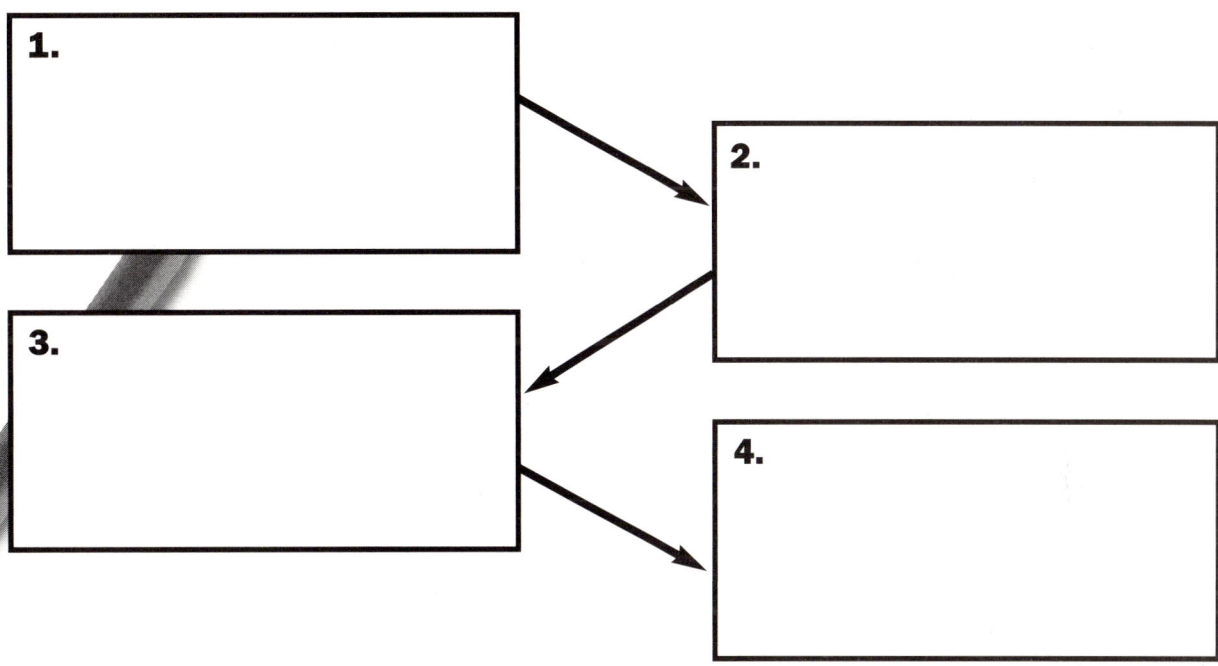

B. Writing Sentences Now write a short draft of your story. Use extra paper if you need more space.

_____
_____
_____
_____

My Summary of the Lesson

LESSON 19 • WRITING A STORY **101**

Name _____

FOR USE WITH PAGES 292–299

Understanding Adjectives and Adverbs

My Word List

A. Definition Chart Complete the Definition Chart below.

Word	Definition
modify	
comparative	
superlative	
adjective	
adverb	

B. Labeling Sentence Parts Tell whether the underlined word is an adjective or an adverb.

1. _____ The boy whistled <u>happily</u> while he worked.
2. _____ The mother was <u>sad</u> to see her daughter leave home.
3. _____ Maria is 3 inches <u>taller</u> than her sister Margarita.
4. _____ The test seemed quite <u>hard</u>.
5. _____ My grandmother makes the <u>best</u> cookies in the world!

Skill Building

A. Combining Sentences Combine each pair of sentences into one sentence.

1. Esmeralda Santiago was born in a small town. The town is in Puerto Rico.
_____

2. Santiago moved from Puerto Rico to New York City. She was 13 years old when she moved. _____

3. Santiago wrote *Almost a Woman*. She also wrote *When I Was Puerto Rican* and *America's Dream*. _____

4. Santiago remembers her childhood. She remembers it clearly.
_____

5. As an adult, Santiago has written many books. Her books are about her life.
_____

B. Writing Sentences Write your own sentences using the adjective or adverb provided.

1. messy: _____

2. faster: _____

3. angrily: _____

4. too: _____

5. best: _____

My Study Notes

A. Study Skill: Adjective and Adverb Chart Complete the Adjective and Adverb Chart. Make each word comparative and superlative.

Word	Comparative	Superlative
happy		
loudly		
slow		
messy		
good		
fast		
black		
strong		

B. Key Details Match the definitions with the underlined words they describe.

1. Santiago is my favorite author.
2. I read her books and write about them in my journal.
3. My friend from school likes to read under the tree in my yard.
4. Her second book is better, but the third one is the best.

- adjective phrases
- nouns
- irregular comparative adjectives
- verbs

104 ACCESS ENGLISH

Lesson 20

Name

FOR USE WITH PAGE 300

Showing What I Know

Interpreting Read the selection from *Almost a Woman* below and circle the adjectives and adjective phrases. Put a box around the adverb phrases.

"New York was darker than I expected, and, in spite of the cleansing rain, dirtier. Used to the sensual curves of rural Puerto Rico, my eyes had to adjust to the regular, aggressive two-dimensionality of Brooklyn. Raindrops pounded the hard streets, captured the dim silver glow of street lamps, bounced against sidewalks in glistening sparks, then disappeared, like tiny ephemeral jewels, into the darkness."

Now try to interpret the meaning of the selection. How does Santiago describe her first impression of New York? Use the adjectives and adverbs as clues to help you interpret the meaning.

_____
_____
_____
_____
_____
_____
_____

My Summary of the Lesson

LESSON 20 • UNDERSTANDING ADJECTIVES AND ADVERBS

Theme 6: Making a Difference

Theme

A. List and Define The people shown on page 302 of *ACCESS English* all made a difference in our world. List 5 words that come to mind when you think about making a difference in the world. Define each word.

1. _____
2. _____
3. _____
4. _____
5. _____

B. Using a Web If you could change one thing in this world to help others, what would it be? What are some of the things you could do to help? Complete the Web below.

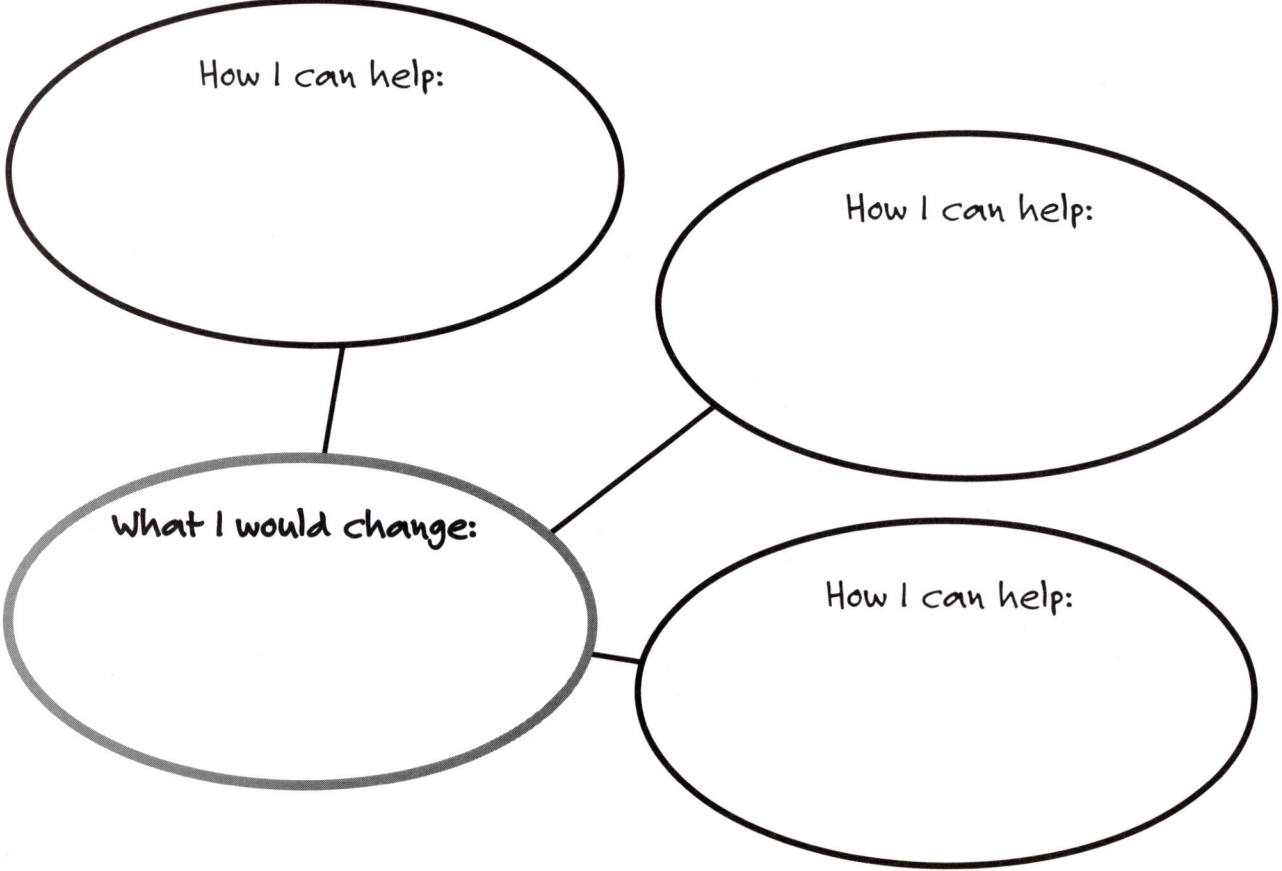

Name

FOR USE WITH PAGE 303

Literary Element

A. Definition Chart Use page 303 of *ACCESS English* to complete the Definition Chart below.

Word	Definition	Example Sentence
author's purpose		
clues		

B. Writing Sentences As you read the selection, ask yourself what is the author's purpose for writing "Lessons of Dr. Martin Luther King, Jr."? Use the chart on page 303 of *ACCESS English* to help you answer.

Literature Connection

Using a Web to Explain Read pages 304–305 of *ACCESS English*. How did Dr. Martin Luther King, Jr., make a difference? Complete the Web with a difference he made and examples of how he did it.

Name _____

FOR USE WITH PAGE 306

Learn About Literature

Connotation and Denotation List 5 words from "Lessons of Dr. Martin Luther King, Jr.," that you think have a connotation. Tell whether the connotation is positive or negative. Then look up the denotation of the word in the dictionary. Write it in the last column.

Word	Connotation	Denotation
1.		
2.		
3.		
4.		
5.		
6.		

My Summary of the Lesson

Name _____

FOR USE WITH PAGES 310–317

Reading Real-world Writing

My Word List

A. Definitions For each vocabulary word, write the definition in the box next to it. Use the Key Concepts on page 310 of *ACCESS English* if you need help.

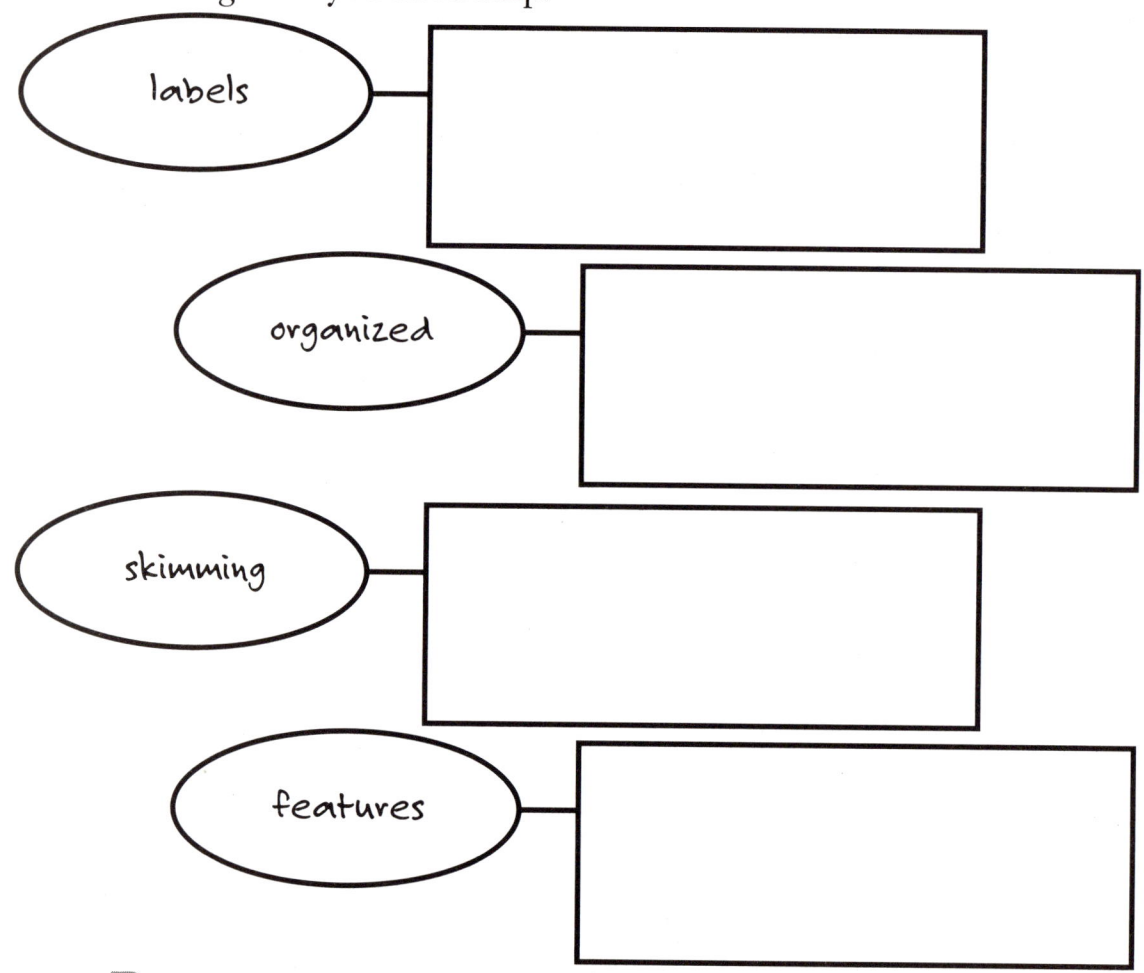

B. Sentence Frames Use the vocabulary words from above to complete these sentences.

1. In real-world writing, _____ are often used like titles or headings.
2. To find information quickly, try _____ the text.
3. Pay attention to how the text is _____.
4. Bulleted items, headings, and graphics are some _____ found in real-world writing.

110 ACCESS ENGLISH

Lesson 21

Name _____

FOR USE WITH PAGE 311

Skill Building

A. **Skimming** Skim the party invitation below. Highlight or underline key words.

COME TO MY PARTY!

Looking for something to do this weekend? I'm having a party! There will be food, fun, and dancing. It will be a great time! Please come, and feel free to bring a friend! Party begins at 7:00 P.M.

Where: 2 Bliss St.
When: Saturday, May 27
R.S.V.P. by Wednesday!

B. **Finding Information** For each type of real-world writing, tell what things you would look for if you were skimming it.

1. A how-to manual: _____

2. A train schedule: _____

3. A flyer for a school play: _____

4. A menu: _____

5. A map: _____

LESSON 21 • READING REAL-WORLD WRITING 111

Name _____

FOR USE WITH PAGES 312–317

My Study Notes

A. Study Skill: Outlining Steps Complete the outline of the lesson. Use pages 312–317 of *ACCESS English* if you need help.

1. Four Steps for Reading Real-world Writing
   a. _____
   b. _____
   c. _____
   d. _____

2. Tips for Reading Schedules
   a. _____
   b. _____
   c. _____

3. Tips for Reading Instructions
   a. _____
   b. _____
   c. _____
   d. _____
   e. _____
   f. _____

Word Bank

schedule

map

manual

context clues

instructions

B. Key Details Use the Word Bank to complete these sentences.

1. The how-to _____ shows the correct way to install the car stereo.
2. The _____ says a train arrives every 20 minutes.
3. The _____ shows that we are 20 miles from our home.
4. Follow the _____ for putting together the bookcase.
5. Look for _____ to help you understand the meaning of a new word.

Lesson 21

Name _____

FOR USE WITH PAGE 318

Showing What I Know

A. Comparing and Contrasting Find two pieces of real-world writing that describe the same thing in different ways. For example, you might choose two menus, schedules, or sets of directions for how to get to the same place. Use the Venn Diagram to compare and contrast them.

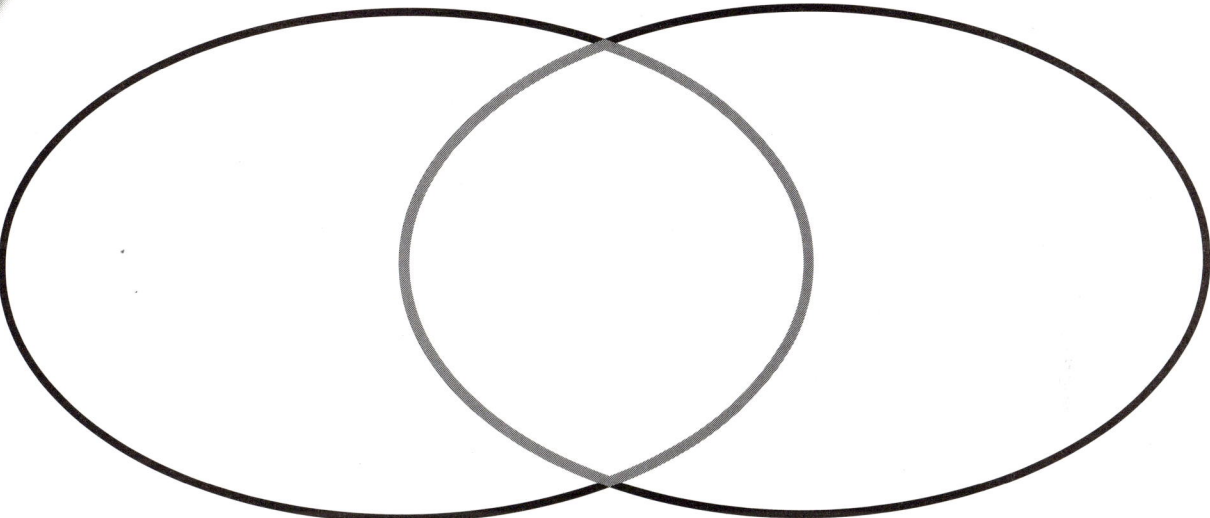

B. Writing Sentences Use the information from your Venn Diagram to compare how the two pieces of real-world writing are alike and how they are different.

_____
_____
_____
_____

My Summary of the Lesson

LESSON 21 • READING REAL-WORLD WRITING

Persuasive Writing

My Word List

A. Writing Sentences Write a sentence for each word that explains its connection to persuasive writing.

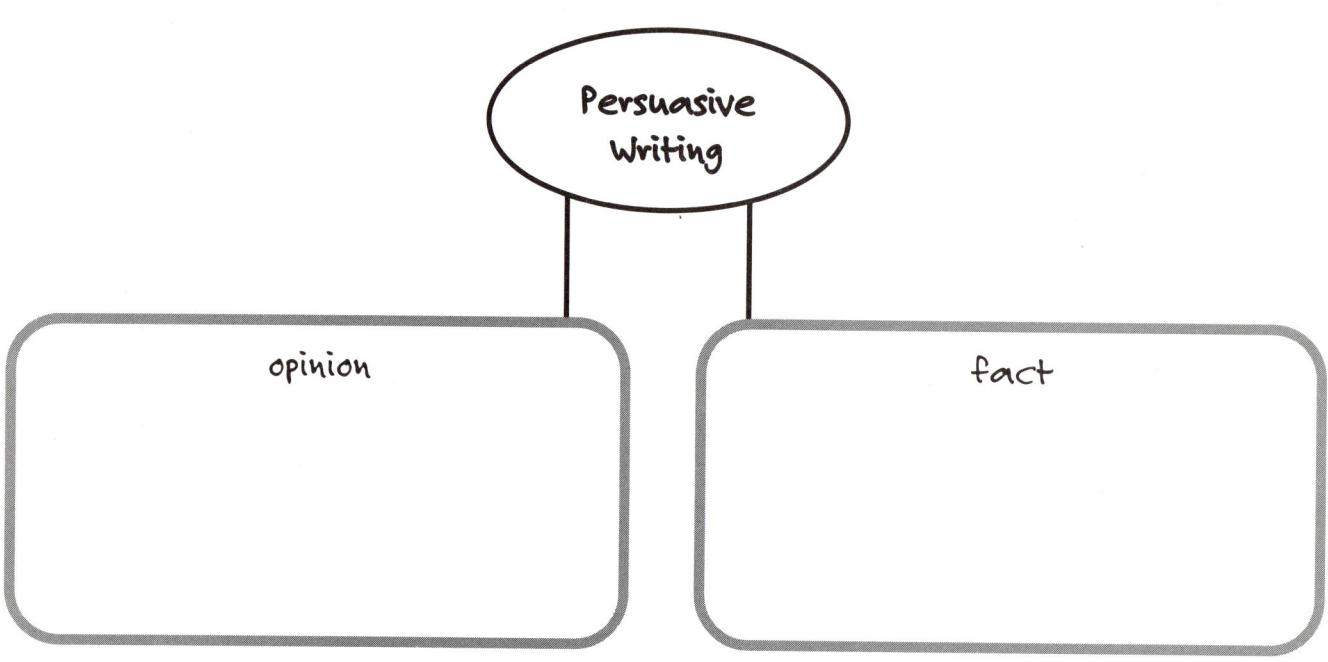

B. Sentence Frames Use the words from the organizer above to complete these sentences.

1. Throughout history, people have used _____ to change the way others think about important social issues.

2. In the 1960s, almost everyone had a strong _____ about civil rights.

3. Both men wrote powerful speeches that were full of strong emotion but based on _____.

Name _____

Lesson 22

FOR USE WITH PAGE 323

Skill Building

A. **Supporting an Opinion** Complete the Opinion Organizer with a subject, an opinion you have about that subject, and 3 details to support your opinion.

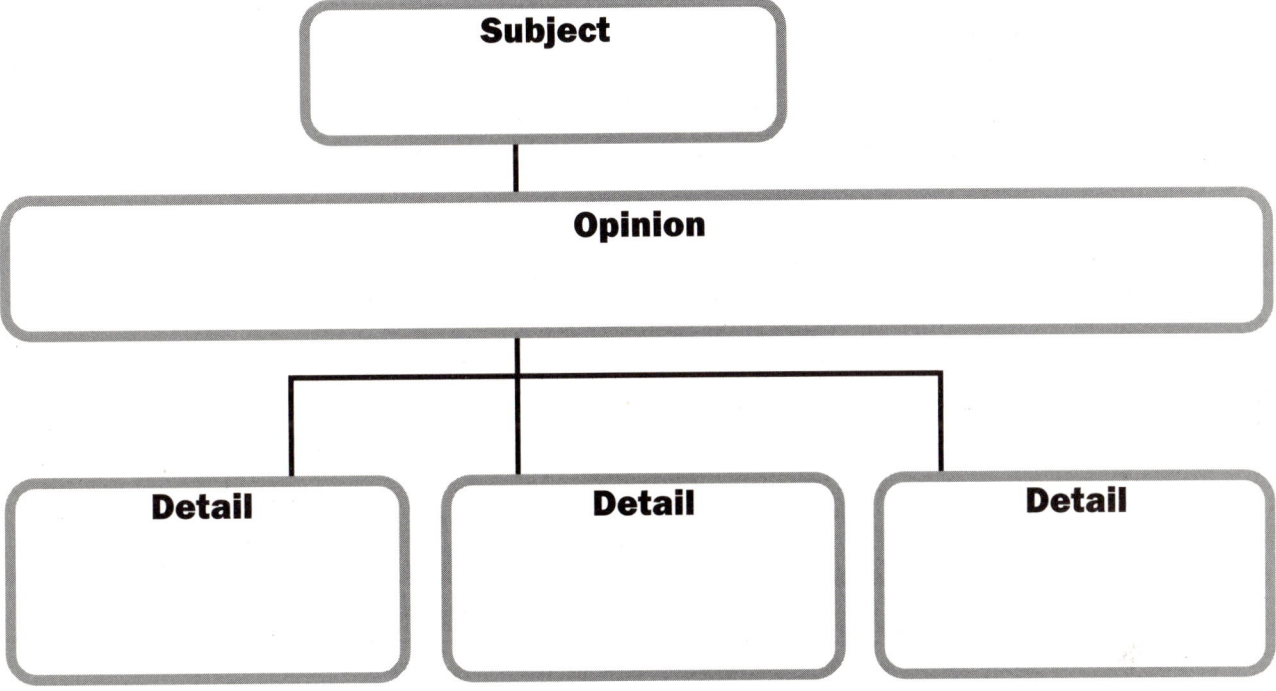

B. **Writing Sentences** Use the Opinion Organizer to write a paragraph supporting your opinion.

_____
_____
_____
_____
_____
_____
_____
_____

Name

FOR USE WITH PAGES 324–329

My Study Notes

A. Study Skill: Outlining the Lesson Complete the study outline for this lesson. For sections 1 and 2, describe what each heading means.

1. Kinds of Persuasive Writing
   a.
   b.
   c.
   d.

2. Three Parts of an Argument
   a.
   b.
   c.

3. Writing a Persuasive Argument
   a.
   b.
   c.
   d.
   e.

B. Key Details Use the Word Bank to complete these sentences.

1. Another word for opinion is _____.
2. One purpose for persuasive writing is to support or promote an important _____.
3. A good way to strengthen your argument is to address _____ viewpoints.
4. A letter of _____ persuades someone to fix a problem.
5. In your writing, try to address possible _____ to your opinion.

Word Bank
viewpoint
objections
complaint
cause
opposing

116 ACCESS ENGLISH

Name

Lesson 22

FOR USE WITH PAGE 330

Showing What I Know

A. **Persuading** Choose a topic you have a strong opinion about. Complete the Persuasive Paragraph Organizer.

Topic	Viewpoint	Support for Viewpoint
		1.
		2.
	Opposing Viewpoint	3.
		4.

B. **Persuading Others** Use the information in your Persuasive Paragraph Organizer to write a paragraph in which you try to persuade a reader to agree with you.

_____
_____
_____
_____
_____
_____

My Summary of the Lesson

LESSON 22 • PERSUASIVE WRITING

Writing Letters

My Word List

A. Definition Chart Complete the Definition Chart below.

Word	Definition	Example Sentence
formal		
informal		
audience		
purpose		
email		

B. Sentence Frames Use words from above to fill in the blanks.

When writing a letter, think about who will read it. Is your _____ a friend? If so, your letter can be _____. What if your _____ is to address a business? You would need to write a _____ letter. If you do not have time to send a letter, an _____ is a fast way to send a message.

Skill Building

Proofreading Your Writing Use proofreader's marks to correct the letter below. Refer to the Letter-writing Checklist on page 335 of *ACCESS English* to help you.

2 Bliss Street
Marlboro, ma 02754
August 10 2004

sunshine summer camp
2020 Willow Avenue
Salem MA 02700

Dear director Adams:

I am replying to your ad in the <u>weekly times</u>. I think that I am well qualified for position of camp counselor. i love children and I was in the Girl Scouts for 5 years. I think I would be a terrific counselor.

Please consider my application. I look forward to speaking with you more about this position.

Sincerely,
Greta Smith

Name

FOR USE WITH PAGES 336–341

My Study Notes

A. Study Skills: Key Word or Topic Notes Name and describe the 5 parts of a friendly letter and tell what they are. See page 337 in *ACCESS English*.

Key Words	Notes
heading	
greeting	
body	
closing	
signature	

B. Key Details Use the Word Bank to complete these sentences.

Word Bank
sincerely
salutation
recommendation
issues
complaint

1. She signed her letter "_____, Laura."

2. This cereal tastes so awful that I am going to write a letter of _____ to the company.

3. I made a _____ to recycle at my school.

4. Tomás and I exchanged a brief _____ when we passed each other in the hallway.

5. Student council meetings are a place for students to talk about important _____ at school.

Lesson 23

Name _____

FOR USE WITH PAGE 342

Showing What I Know

A. Responding   Think of an issue that is important to you. Use the Web to organize your thoughts and respond to the issue.

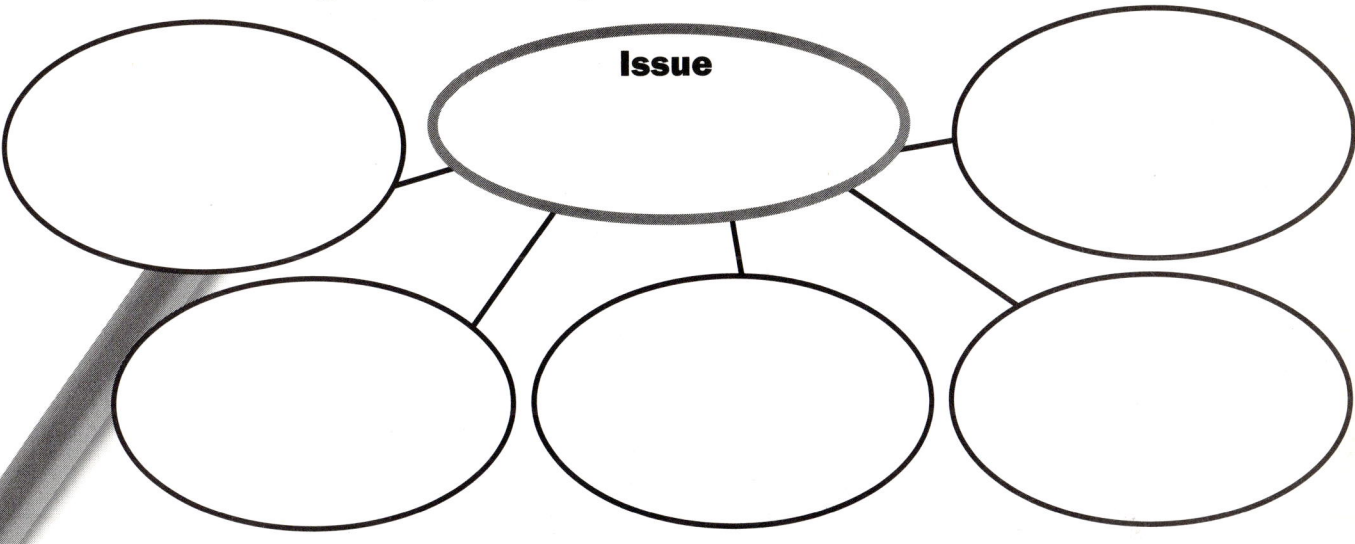

B. Writing a Letter   Write a letter of opinion that responds to the issue you chose above. Remember to address it to someone. Your audience could be newspaper readers, a politician, or a business.

_____
_____
_____
_____
_____
_____

My Summary of the Lesson

More Parts of Speech

My Word List

A. Definition Chart Complete the Definition Chart below.

Word	Definition	Example
parts of speech		
function		
gender		
masculine		
feminine		

B. Sentence Frames Use the Definition Chart to complete the sentences.

1. *He* is a _____ subject pronoun.
2. The _____ pronoun *she* can be used to replace a woman's name in a sentence.
3. Prepositions are _____ that show relationship or location.
4. The _____ of a conjunction is to connect words or groups of words.
5. The _____ of the word *it* is neuter.

Name

Lesson 24

FOR USE WITH PAGE 347

Skill Building

Building Vocabulary In the spaces below, write 5 words you heard but do not already know. Follow steps 3–5 and the model on page 347 of *ACCESS English* for each word.

1. Word:
   Definition:
   Sentence:

2. Word:
   Definition:
   Sentence:

3. Word:
   Definition:
   Sentence:

4. Word:
   Definition:
   Sentence:

5. Word:
   Definition:
   Sentence:

Name _____

FOR USE WITH PAGES 348–353

My Study Notes

A. Study Skills: Outlining the Lesson Complete the list of parts of speech discussed in this lesson. Tell what each part of speech does.

Parts of Speech
1. Pronouns:
    a.
    b.
    c.

2. Prepositions:

3. Conjunctions:

4. Interjections:

B. Key Details Use words from the Word Bank to complete these sentences.

Word Bank
person
case
neuter
modifiers
prepositional phrase

1. *You* is a second _____ pronoun.
2. When a pronoun replaces a noun that has no gender, it is called _____.
3. Adjectives or adverbs are _____ that are used to limit the meaning of another word.
4. *On the rusted gate* is an example of a _____.
5. The _____ of a personal pronoun shows whether it is a subject, object, or possessive pronoun.

124 ACCESS ENGLISH

Lesson 24

Name

FOR USE WITH PAGE 354

Showing What I Know

A. Persuading Should there be curfews for teenagers? Use the Argument Chart below to help you form your argument.

Viewpoint	3 Supporting Details	Opposing Viewpoint	Answer
	1.		
	2.		
	3.		

B. Writing Sentences Now write your persuasive argument below.

_____
_____
_____
_____
_____
_____
_____

My Summary of the Lesson

LESSON 24 • MORE PARTS OF SPEECH

Writing Resources
PROOFREADER'S MARKS

HOW TO MARK	MEANING	EXAMPLE
≡	Capitalize a letter.	francisco jiménez wrote "The Circuit."
/	Make a capital letter lowercase.	Yoshiko and Keiko were Sisters.
⊙	Insert a period.	Pat Mora is a writer and teacher⊙ She wrote "Immigrants."
sp.	Correct the spelling.	Their are three steps in the reading process. (sp. There)
⌒	Take out or delete.	Adjectives are words that that describe nouns.
∧	Insert here.	Harriet Tubman made 19 trips to ∧South. (the)
¶	Start a new paragraph.	¶The first sentence in a paragraph should always be indented. This helps the writer signal a new main idea.

Practice Use proofreader's marks to correct the sentences.

1. Panchito speaks Spanish. Mr. lema helps him speak the english.

2. in "Saying Yes," Diana chang talks about being Chinese annd American.

3. Esperanza'z grandmother was a strong Woman, born in the year of horse.

4. Maniac magee thought Amanda was runing away from home because she carried a suitcase.

5. Yoshiko her family celebrated Obon in japan

6. When was the Great Migration

7. César Chávez grew up california. He worked as migrant worker and fought four better working conditions.

8. Chávez led protests against companies that did not treat workers fairly chávez was inspired by Dr. Martin Luther King, Jr.

Name

FIXING SENTENCE FRAGMENTS AND RUN-ON SENTENCES

Sentence Parts Remember that a sentence has two main parts: the subject and the predicate.

Panchito <u>*worked in the fields.*</u> *Panchito and his family* <u>*moved to find work.*</u>
SUBJECT   PREDICATE   SUBJECT   PREDICATE

Sentence Fragments A sentence fragment is not a complete sentence. A fragment is missing a subject or a predicate.

Fragment	Complete Sentence
Worked in the fields.	Panchito worked in the fields.

Run-on Sentences A run-on sentence is two more sentences put together without the correct punctuation or connecting words.

Run-on	Complete Sentences
Panchito's family worked in the fields and they had to move to find work they had a hard life.	Panchito's family worked in the fields. They had to move to find work, and they had a hard life.

Practice Fix each fragment and run-on below.

1. Felt like a foreigner in Japan.

_____

_____

2. Duke Ellington was an important jazz musician, he played the piano.

_____

_____

3. Everyone in Esperanza's family has different hair, Esperanza says her hair is "lazy," it doesn't obey barrettes.

_____

_____

4. Offered to teach Panchito how to play the trumpet.

_____

COMBINING SENTENCES

When you combine sentences, you turn short sentences into one smoother, more interesting sentence. Combine sentences using phrases, key words, or connecting words, such as *and*, *or*, or *but*.

and	connects two ideas that are alike
or	gives a choice
but	shows contrast

Forming Compound Sentences

Two Sentences	Combined Sentence
Yoshiko stayed at a rural inn. She ate dinner outside on the veranda.	Yoshiko stayed at a rural inn, and she ate dinner outside on the veranda.
A woman asked Yoshiko to read a sign. Yoshiko couldn't read Japanese.	A woman asked Yoshiko to read a sign, but Yoshiko couldn't read Japanese.

Combining Key Words or Phrases

Sentences	Combined Sentence
Yoshiko ate miso soup. She ate broiled eel. She ate bean paste cakes.	Yoshiko ate miso soup, broiled eel, and bean paste cakes.
Yoshiko heard the cicadas. They were buzzing in unison.	Yoshiko heard the cicadas buzzing in unison.

Practice Combine each group of sentences to form one sentence.

1. Cathy is Esperanza's neighbor. She is not very friendly.

___

2. Mr. Lema was patient. He was helpful. He was kind.

___

3. Martin's grandpa got off the bus. He got off at Bell View Drive.

___

4. Malcolm X inspired many people. He left the United States a better place.

___